COUNTDOWN TO GCSE
FRENCH
AND
GERMAN

Gillian Taylor

Previous Head of French,
Henry Beaufort School, Winchester;
currently Director of Phoenix Tutors

**MACMILLAN
EDUCATION**

First published 1986

Published by
MACMILLAN EDUCATION LTD
Houndmills, Basingstoke, Hampshire RG21 2XS
and London
Companies and representatives
throughout the world

Typeset by TecSet Ltd,
Sutton, Surrey
Printed in Great Britain by
Cox & Wyman Ltd
Reading

Designed and illustrated by
Plum Design
Southampton

British Library Cataloguing in Publication Data
Taylor, Gillian
French and German.–(Countdown to GCSE)
I. Title II. Series
448   PC2112
ISBN 0–333–40950–7

CONTENTS

Countdown to GCSE: French and German

ACKNOWLEDGEMENTS

The author and publishers wish to acknowledge the following sources:

Thomas Nelson & Sons Ltd for extract from *Deutsch Heute Teil I* by Duncan Sidwell and Penny Capoore; Oxford University Press for extract from *Communications* by David Sprake (1981); *De Telegraaf* for extracts from *De Telegraaf*, February 1985; Times Newspapers Ltd for extracts from *The Times*, June 1984 and extracts from *The Times Educational Supplement*, January 1984; also
London and East Anglia Group; Northern Examining Association; Southern Examining Group; University of Cambridge Local Examinations Syndicate.

The publishers have made every effort to trace the copyright holders, but if they have inadvertently overlooked any, they will be pleased to make the necessary arrangements at the first opportunity.

INTRODUCTION

This book is for the lucky young people who will be taking GCSE in a foreign language, and for their parents. Lucky? Yes, lucky to benefit from the most sweeping reforms ever known in language exams in this country.

For parents

Whether or not you have ever studied the language yourself, you can support your children by understanding what they have to do and how they can best prepare. Section 1 and the first part of Section 2 provide general information for non-specialists. If you *have* taken language exams, or have seen older children through CSE or 'O' level, you may find that your child doesn't seem to know facts which were always drilled in the past. This book will help you judge whether you have cause for concern. In fact, as you read on, you may well be more worried if your child *is* being taught in the same way as earlier generations!

For candidates

It's hard to take aim if you can't see the target. Once you know what's expected of you, you can take calm, confident steps to achieve it.

This book *doesn't* attempt to contain all the language facts you need to know. GCSE isn't simply an exam in *how much* you know — it's a course in *using* what you know. School text-books have all the verb tables and vocabulary lists you need.

This book *is* about applying your knowledge with skill and thought and common sense. It helps you to exploit the school resources to your best advantage, and to understand your syllabus, so that you can sort out priorities in learning.

Apart from the sections on French and German and some of the exam practice tasks, the book applies to Spanish, Italian and Russian as well as to French and German.

SECTION I

About the exam

GCSE: THE NEED FOR THE NEW EXAM

Why has GCSE (the General Certificate of Secondary Education) replaced 'O' level and CSE?

New Certificate to replace 'O' level and CSE exams
The Times, 21 June 1984

Reform in all subjects

'O' level was passed by approximately the top 20% of the population. Candidates never knew exactly what they had to do to be sure of a pass; they just had to be better than about 80% of sixteen year olds in the country. Picture the MOT test being run in the same way:

Mechanic: Sorry sir, I can't pass your car.

Owner: What's wrong with it?

Mechanic: Not a lot, but you see sir, I can only pass about one in five. We've had a lot in today, and too many of them were better than yours.

Owner: Well, how can I make mine good enough?

Mechanic: It's more than my job's worth to tell you that, sir. Tell you what, try again in six months. We don't get so many in in November, so you might stand a better chance. And you could try a little Brasso on the hub-caps . . .

(Six months later . . .)

Mechanic: Sorry, sir. They're all using that Brasso trick now. Now don't take it personally. It was a good car, and you did your best, but the competition was pretty stiff. Can I interest you in a second-hand bike?

3

'O' level was a sort of club which restricted membership, in order, it was said, to preserve standards. And quite right, too, was the general opinion: an exam which everybody could pass would be meaningless.

Or would it? Think about reading. For centuries, only the privileged few were taught to read. Nobody claims that reading has become meaningless now that anybody can do it! If children thought that only 20% of them could 'pass' reading, many wouldn't try, and national standards would plummet. So why *shouldn't* we come to expect average sixteen year olds to achieve standards formerly intended for only 20% of them? They *need* higher standards. Today's young people will not live in an agricultural nation, nor even an industrial nation, but in an information society. They've got to be educated for it. Look at these quotes from a 1984 speech by the Secretary of State for Education on the short-comings of the old exams:

> In any subject far more pupils than at present should reach the level of knowledge and skill now associated generally with an 'O' level grade C.

> . . . a higher level of attainment at age 16 than the present one for every step of the ability range including those for whom the exist-ing 16-plus examinations are now designed.

> . . . substantially higher standards of attainment at age 16 can be achieved in this country by pupils throughout the ability range.

GCSE plans to set the standards for all to see: no more of the mystery of 'O' level. With grade criteria specified for each individual grade, it will be clear exactly what has to be achieved to gain, say, grade C. The criteria for the grade will not alter, however good or bad the candidates are. If, in later years, more candidates gain higher grades, then national standards will have risen. And the highest grades will still have sufficient rarity value to distinguish the outstanding scholars.

The moral of all this is: you aren't fighting inscrutable examiners. You aren't competing with your friends. So aim high.

Reform in modern languages

In the days when modern languages were taught only in grammar schools, to the academic few, languages were not classed as practical subjects. Cookery students produced edible meals, woodwork students made usable artefacts, but language students did *not* expect to converse with foreigners. An 'O' level was just a beginning, the foothills of achievement up the steep mountain of language learning, a tough climb, but necessary if one were eventually to enjoy the view from the top of the full richness of the foreign culture.

Why? Because university lecturers in modern languages, copying their colleagues in classics, taught literature and translation. So they insisted that literature and translation were begun at 'A' level. This was only possible if literary vocabulary and the grammar needed for translation were taught at 'O' level. And never mind that 'O' level candidates could rarely understand or reply to a native speaker.

The apparent British inability to speak foreign languages became a national joke. As a child on holiday in France, I saw how 'O' level failed my mother: all her knowledge of verb endings didn't help her in a desperate search for public conveniences. 'Pour les dames?' she asked mystified passers-by. It's not the sort of thing you can mime ...

When comprehensives replaced grammar schools, suddenly almost every child was learning a foreign language. Painfully. The new CSE exams introduced in the sixties were watered-down 'O' levels, still academic rather than practical.

Later CSE syllabuses were quite enlightened, introducing role-play, where the pupil acts out being a tourist abroad, and taped listening tests using native speakers. So, ironically, in many schools only the CSE group learnt *useful* language; 'O' level pupils were far too busy cramming grammatical facts which would come in handy provided they continued to study the language for years more. Yet only 'O' level had prestige!

Reform from the chalk face

Pupils voted with their feet: as soon as they were allowed, they flocked away from language classrooms, having acquired little but a sense of failure. Then in the 1970s came an astonishing reaction from teachers: volunteer groups all over Britain devoted countless leisure hours to devising 'graded objectives' schemes to test knowledge of useful, practical language. Originally for less able eleven to fourteen year olds, the certificates were so popular that older, brighter children demanded them too. The tide of reform was washing around the rock of the academic 'O' level, undermining its sacred tenets. Sooner or later it had to crumble.

In 1984, when the Secretary of State for Education decided to scrap 'O' level and CSE, he said:

> . . . the curriculum should be relevant to the real world and to the pupils' experience of it.

No more translations of literary snippets out of context!

> . . . much of what many pupils are now asked to learn is clutter.

No more learning unnecessary grammar just because it exists!

> . . . the curriculum should contain an adequate practical element and promote practical capability for all pupils, not just for those who are labelled 'non-academic' . . .

No more restricting speaking and listening skills to the lower sets!

The GCSE National Criteria document welcomed this chance to 'improve syllabuses and methods of assessment in modern languages' and 'attract a much greater number of candidates'. No longer are you expected to continue your languages: the course is 'appropriate to the needs of a wide variety of candidates', and first on the list are 'those leaving school at sixteen'. It must also suit 'those going on to specialise in the subject'. But whether you stop at sixteen or later, you should take from your years of study not just a certificate but also ready-to-use language skills.

AIMS: WHAT THE COURSE SHOULD DO FOR YOU

This section is to give you an impression of *why* you have to do what you have to do. *What* you have to do is in the next section.

Here are the seven aims of the GCSE National Criteria for modern languages, applying to all candidates in England and Wales.

1 to develop the ability to use languages effectively for purposes of practical communication

Communication: that's aim number one, and perhaps the only purpose of using language at all.

Communication

Non-communication

Moral: grammar isn't much use unless you can say something with it.

2 to form a sound base of the skills, language and attitudes required for further study, work and leisure

Like 'O' level, a GCSE course equips you to continue to study the subject. But unlike 'O' level it will also equip you for leisure or business contacts with the language.

3 to offer insights into the culture and civilisation of French/German-speaking countries

You'll learn about how people think and live, as well as how they speak. Language courses in the past contained no foreign flavour. Real contact with abroad, when it came, was a surprise: all that kissing and shaking hands! What should be ordered in a bar? Whatever was that food? Ignorance causes shock, shock causes fear, fear leads to suspicion; and ignorant fear of foreigners is something we can do without in this shrinking world.

4 to develop an awareness of the nature of language and language learning

While aim **3** encourages awareness of lifestyles, aim **4** encourages awareness of words. The more languages you learn, the more fascinating words become. For instance, you'll have noticed that some French and German words resemble English ones.

English	*German*	*English*	*French*
hand	*Hand*	table	*table*
mouse	*Maus*	beauty	*beauté*

But had you noticed that English words related to German tend to belong to simple, everyday life, and those introduced by the educated, French-speaking, Norman overlords after 1066 are more sophisticated or poetic? Sometimes English has two words with the same meaning, one from German and used in conversation, the other from French and used mostly in writing:

This sort of awareness can do wonders for your written English style. Your course should also train you to notice relationships and patterns between one language and another, so that whatever language you might encounter later, you will be equipped to pick it up as quickly as possible.

5 to provide enjoyment and intellectual stimulation

The amazing thing about this aim is that it's here! You wouldn't have found it on a pre-GCSE syllabus, yet it's very important in view of aim **6**:

6 to encourage positive attitudes to foreign language learning and to speakers of foreign languages, and a sympathetic approach to other cultures and civilisations

You're more likely to think warmly of foreigners if you've found learning their language interesting and enjoyable.

7 to promote learning skills of a more general application (e.g. analysis, memorising, drawing of inferences)

The more work and thought you put into your language learning, the better equipped your mind will be to cope with any other demands put on it, linguistic or otherwise.

So, to sum up, your course should provide you with ready-to-use skills which could be even more useful later on, and give you some interesting and enjoyable glimpses of how other people live and communicate. As a result, you should become a more tolerant citizen of the world, and also a more effective thinker — which can't be bad.

THE EXAM: WHAT'S IN THE TEST PAPERS

Compulsory	*Optional*
*Basic Listening	Basic Writing
Basic Reading	*Higher Listening
Basic Speaking	Higher Reading
	Higher Speaking **
	Higher Writing ***

* The names 'Basic' and 'Higher' may vary from one Examining Group to another.

** Usually the longer 'Higher Speaking' test counts as both 'Basic' and 'Higher', because it is very time-consuming to give two speaking tests to the same candidate.

***You can't take 'Higher Writing' without taking 'Basic Writing' too.

All the tests are based on two principles quoted from the GCSE National Criteria for modern languages. Aim number one of the course is to enable you to 'use the language effectively for purposes of practical communication'; and all tasks must be 'authentic and valuable outside the classroom'. In other words, they must be *useful,* and not purely academic exercises.

There are five examining Groups in England and Wales. Their 'Listening' and 'Reading' tests are all similar, their 'Speaking' tests vary somewhat, and their 'Writing' tests vary a lot. Your teacher has a copy of the syllabus for the Group which your school has chosen, and should let you know just what to expect in the 'Speaking' and 'Writing' tests.

Listening

You'll hear . . .
. . . a 30–45-minute tape consisting of: several dialogues recorded by native speakers, with pauses for thinking and writing.

. . . at 'Higher' level, some ordinary unscripted speech at normal or near-normal speed, perhaps with some natural hesitations and background noise.

The speakers will be . . .
. . . talking on ordinary topics (like school, family, holidays); or acting out everyday situations (shopping, asking the way, etc.).

. . . asking you questions (e.g. 'What's your name?'); giving you information or instructions ('It's not far. Take the second road on the right.'); discussing something, (e.g. where to go); making an announcement ('The train now standing at platform one . . .'); or broadcasting (e.g. weather forecasts).

So . . .
. . . it's *not* your teacher reading aloud. There will be variety (of sex/age, formal announcements/ informal chat, radio broadcasts, phone calls, etc.) as in real life.

. . . there will probably be words you don't understand, as there are in real encounters with other languages. You cope by picking out the words you *do* know.

So . . .
. . . they *won't* be discussing anything unexpected, only those subjects most likely to crop up if you visit the country or meet its people.

. . . they *won't* be reading out literary or old-fashioned texts. They'll be saying the sort of things they would say to you or which you might overhear.

For each taped item, you'll have to . . .

. . . read the English introduction, so that you know where the speakers are and what they are doing.

. . . read the questions so that you know exactly what details to listen out for.

. . . listen twice. In real life, the speaker would see from your expression if you didn't understand, and would repeat or simplify. Since that's impractical in an exam, everything is heard twice instead.

. . . listen out for the words or phrases which answer the question. You may only need to identify a couple of key words (Basic), or you may need to follow the main points of the whole passage and perhaps draw a conclusion (Higher).

. . . (if the questions are in English) answer in your own English words. Give all the relevant information.

. . . sometimes, make a choice (e.g. decide which signpost to follow).

So . . .

. . . you *don't* have to guess the context (as often happened in 'O' level), because in real life, of course, you'd be able to see.

. . . you *don't* have to remember *everything* you hear, only the specific information which has been asked for.

. . . *don't* panic on the first hearing. It's *not* a test of memory. Long texts may be repeated a third time or broken into shorter chunks during the repeat, or you may make notes.

. . . there's *no need* to understand *every* word, as long as you catch the key points asked for in the question.

. . . you *don't* answer in French/German; this isn't a writing test. You *don't* have to write in full sentences — note form will do; this isn't a test of English.

. . . multiple choice questions will usually only be used in situations where you would have a choice in real life.

•

Reading

You'll see . . .

. . . between ten and twenty texts of varying lengths and on various topics, perhaps with diagrams, drawings, photos, maps and so on.

. . . texts written *by* native speakers *for* native speakers. They may be shortened or slightly simplified (Basic), but very often, especially at 'Higher' level, they will be unedited and authentic.

The reading texts are . . .

. . . on the same everyday topics as those for 'Speaking' (page 16).

. . . sources of information (e.g. timetables); interest (e.g. tourist brochures); pleasure (e.g. magazine articles); or communication (e.g. letters).

For each text, you'll have to . . .

. . . read the English introduction, so that you know where the original came from — just as in real life you'd know if you were handling a crisp packet, or a newspaper, a love letter, or whatever.

. . . read the questions so that you know exactly what details to look out for. You can then skim through longer texts to find the relevant sections. (Look for clues in the layout as shown on page 74.)

So . . .

. . . there *won't* be just one or two long passages, as there used to be in 'O' level, when candidates could get stuck for the whole test through not understanding one key word.

. . . the texts are *not* written by British examiners for British candidates. There may be words which you've never met. Coping with the unknown, as you would have to in real life, is part of the skill being examined.

So . . .

. . . they are *not* items of purely academic interest.

. . . they *are* the sort of material you need to understand if you travel abroad or receive a letter in the foreign language.

So . . .

. . . you *don't* have to work out what the context is. This helps a lot, because you *know* what sort of thing you'd expect to read on a crisp packet, in a newspaper, etc.

. . . you *don't* always have to read every word. As in real life, you skim until you reach what concerns you, and only then study each word.

. . . identify the words or phrases which answer the questions. As in 'Listening', you may only need to understand a few key words (Basic), or you may need to follow the main points of the whole text, and perhaps draw a conclusion from them (Higher).

. . . you *won't* have to explain every word. The ability to select relevant specific information is one of the skills being tested.

. . . usually answer the questions in English in your own words.

. . . you *don't* have to write full sentences — just convey all relevant information clearly.

. . . sometimes make a choice (for instance, read an entertainments guide, then select a film).

. . . multiple choice questions will normally only be used where a choice exists in real life.

Speaking

All 'Speaking' tests include conversation and role-play, although different exam Groups give them different names. Some may also include extra tasks.

Who is the examiner?

You will be tested and marked either by a visiting examiner or by your teacher. If it's your teacher, your test will be taped, or possibly observed by another teacher. This is to monitor the teacher's consistency in questioning and marking, not to judge *you* twice. It's a fair system, with the advantage that you talk to someone who knows you and what you're interested in, without the disadvantage that your teacher's opinion of you as a person might affect the way he or she judges your performance.

What is 'conversation'?

It's more of an interview than a conversation, since the tester asks all the questions. Some exam Groups instruct examiners to concentrate on specified topics, such as your holidays, or leisure activities, or family; others want free conversation. Either way, you'll only have to talk about subjects in the list on page 17. It's assumed that you've had practice in chatting about all of them beforehand. You're there to talk, so try not to be shy or dull. On the other hand, you *aren't* supposed to natter meaninglessly or recite irrelevant speeches which you've learnt by heart. At 'Higher' level the conversation is to be 'sustained', which means that you should have more to say; perhaps explain how you feel on various matters, and why. Conversation is a social skill as well as a linguistic one, and useful training for careers interviews.

What is 'role-play'?
You are given a card which tells you, in English and/or through pictures and diagrams:

> where to pretend that you are (e.g. in a restaurant/a street/ a family home);

> what part your teacher is playing (e.g. a foreign waiter/passer-by/ teenager);

> what you have to say or ask (e.g. order coffee/ask the way to the station/find out what sport he enjoys).

For 'Basic', you have two role-play cards, with three or more instructions on each. At 'Higher' level, you may have extra cards and you may have to cope with the unexpected. For instance, the card tells you to ask the hotel receptionist for a single room for two nights. At 'Basic' level, the examiner may simply answer, 'Certainly, sir/madam.' At 'Higher', the reply may be: 'We've only got a single for one night. But you can have a double for two nights. What do you want to do?' What happens next is up to you: you might ask whether the double costs more, or say that you'll try another hotel, or anything that's suitable in the circumstances.

What else?
Some Groups include extra tasks, especially at 'Higher' level. You may have to look at pictures or photos and say what has happened in them, or look at drawings, advertisements or menus and answer questions about them.

How long does the test last?
From five to fifteen minutes, depending on the Group. There is also preparation time: you prepare your role-play cards while the previous candidate is being tested.

How well do I have to speak?
Your pronunciation, accent and intonation have to be good enough for a native speaker to understand you *if he or she tries* (Basic) or to understand you *easily* (Higher). At 'Basic' level, you can get full marks provided your message is complete and intelligible, even if it's not perfect. At 'Higher', you must not only convey complete messages, but also use reasonably correct and appropriate language.

Writing
What tasks are set?
There has been fierce controversy about what to include, and no two exam Groups set the same combination of tasks.

These are the commonest tasks:

Basic
Write brief notes or lists (e.g. shopping lists, places to visit);
and/or
write a short message or a post-card;
and/or
write a letter, probably informal but possibly formal.

Higher
Write an informal letter;
and/or
write a formal letter;
and/or
something else.

What are 'informal letters'?

These are letters to imaginary penfriends. You start and end with standard phrases learnt by heart. In the middle you write on subjects from the list overleaf, usually from the conversation topics: yourself, your environment, your experiences and feelings, and the penfriend's. You are told what subjects to write about, but the wording is your own.

What are 'formal letters'?

These are 'Dear Sir' letters. Again, you are told what to write about and you choose the words yourself, but it's even more important to know the beginning and ending formulae. The subject-matter is again from the list on page 16, usually from the role-play settings: writing to reserve seats or accommodation, to report an incident, to complain, and so on.

What is 'something else'?

You may have to look at pictures and relate what happened in them. You may face a task designed to make you jump through grammatical hoops. You may have something completely different. Whatever you have to do, the syllabus issued by your school's exam Group has the details, so it won't be a surprise.

How much do I have to write?

Not much. 'Basic' level usually has one task requiring fewer than 100 words, often in note or list form, and another asking for about 100 words. 'Higher' level sets two or three tasks, needing about 130 words each, and the writing should be in complete sentences.

How well do I have to write?

At 'Basic', a sympathetic native reader should be able to *understand* you. Most, or even all, of the marks are for this. You could sometimes get full marks even if you include errors, provided they aren't the kinds of mistakes which prevent comprehension. A word of caution, however: *you* can't tell which of your mistakes will prevent comprehension and which won't, because *you* know what you mean. It's obviously better *not* to include any mistakes if possible.

At 'Higher', marks will be divided between *communication* (your message must be complete and easily understood); and *quality* (whether the words and phrases you have chosen are the best ones for the job, and how good your spelling, punctuation and grammar are).

THE SYLLABUS: HOW MUCH THERE IS TO LEARN

Settings and topics

Each of the five examining Groups in England and Wales provides a list of settings and topics, showing just what subject-matter may occur in the exam.

The *survival settings* meet the most vital linguistic needs of a visitor abroad. They are situations in which you have to:

speak to ask for or give information;
listen and react to the replies;
read any documents likely to be seen in the circumstances;
write where appropriate, for instance letters giving or asking for information or services.

The *conversation topics* cover personal information. You have to:

speak about yourself (your experiences, your environment, your opinions);
write the same things down in a letter to a penfriend;
listen to someone telling you similar details about himself or herself;
read such accounts if they are written, for instance in a letter or a teenage magazine.

SURVIVAL (ROLE-PLAY) SETTINGS

visiting	acting as host or guest; meeting, greeting, introducing, thanking
sightseeing	obtaining tourist information, finding the way
eating	where and what to eat
travelling	using public transport
driving	using private transport
shopping	finding shops, buying goods, prices
going out	making arrangements to meet
mail and money	phoning, sending mail, changing money
accommodation	finding somewhere to stay

illness	describing symptoms and accidents, getting treatment
lost property	describing what has been lost and how
language	coping with foreign language problems

CONVERSATION TOPICS

people	name, age, appearance of yourself, friends and family
leisure	hobbies, sports, music, going out
home	address, your house and home town, daily routine
weather	and seasons and dates
holidays	past and future, trips abroad
work	school, careers, jobs in the family
opinions	your likes and dislikes, and reasons for them

Speaking

For each setting and topic there are a number of set tasks, from which your exam tasks will be selected. They are listed in great detail in the Groups' syllabuses. To give you the flavour, here is a snippet from one of them (Northern Examining Association):

BASIC LEVEL

14 EDUCATION AND FUTURE CAREER

Candidates should be able to:

Exchange information and opinions about: their present school (where applicable) and its facilities; daily routines (when school begins and ends; how many lessons there are and how long they last; break times and lunch times; homework); school year and holidays; subjects studied (including preferences); opportunities for recreational or sporting activities, and trips.

HIGHER LEVEL

14 EDUCATION AND FUTURE CAREER

Candidates should be able to:

Discuss what sort of education they have had or propose to continue with, at what types of educational institution.

Discuss their plans and hopes for the future, including their plans for the coming months, for the time after completion of their formal education, where they would like to work, giving reasons as appropriate.

Section 2 of this book shows you how to prepare for such tasks (see page 23).

Grammar

The Groups also list the grammar you need to know. What it amounts to is that you need to know enough to express yourself correctly in the 'Speaking' tasks and write the same things down. Section 2 also guides you on the essential grammar points.

Vocabulary

Lastly, the Groups provide lists of the two or three thousand words which you should be able to say or write if need be, plus a few which you are only expected to remember the meanings of. Some words not on the list may also appear in the 'Listening' and 'Reading' tests, because some unscripted speech and authentic documents are used, and you can't expect native speakers to stick to the vocabulary listed on your local syllabus. So there's no point in trying to learn the list. Instead, use Section 2 of this book to become aware of the *kinds* of words you need to know, and build your own collection, in your head or on paper or both.

A copy of the syllabus

The exam Groups' published syllabuses are of almost no practical use to candidates. If you'd like to see one nevertheless, you could ask to see your teacher's copy; it's not a classified, top secret document. If you know which examining Group your school has chosen, you could write for your own copy. Specimen papers are available from the same addresses.

> *Northern Examining Association*, Joint Matriculation Board, Manchester M15 6EU
>
> *Midland Examining Group*, University of Cambridge Local Examinations Syndicate, Syndicate Buildings, 1 Hills Road, Cambridge CB1 2EU
>
> *London and East Anglia Examining Group*, University of London School Examinations Board, Stewart House, 32 Russell Square, London WC1B 5DN
>
> *Southern Examining Group*, University of Oxford Delegacy of Local Examinations, Ewert Place, Summertown, Oxford OX2 7BZ
>
> *Welsh Joint Education Committee*, 245 Western Avenue, Cardiff CF5 2YX

GCSE GRADES: WHAT THEY MEAN AND HOW TO GAIN THEM

The GCSE grades in all subjects go from A to G. Candidates who don't do well enough for Grade G are Ungraded. The new grades correspond broadly to the old 'O' level and CSE grades.

For the next few years, the equivalents with the old qualifications will interest parents, employers and educators who want a basis of comparison. Eventually, though, comparing the two will be as pointless as working out that 67p used to be about 13s 4d, because the meaning of the values will change: 67p doesn't buy what 13s 4d bought. 'I've got French "O" level grade C,' meant 'I'm better at French than about 80% of my age group', whereas 'I've got French GCSE grade C,' will indicate precisely what the candidate had to know and do, and how well. This will come about when the proposed 'grade criteria', which will define the level of attainment for each skill for each grade, have been incorporated into the GCSE marking scheme.

'O' level	*CSE*	*GCSE*
A		A
B } 'pass'	} 1	B
C		C
D } 'fail'	2	D
E	3	E
	4	F
	5	G

GCSE grades in modern languages

It's a pick-and-mix exam, where you can cash in on your strengths by taking the tests which suit you best. The only rule is that you must take 'Basic Listening', 'Basic Reading' and 'Basic Speaking'.

If this is all you attempt, you *may* gain grades G, F or E, depending on how well you do. But for grade E you'll need pretty high scores. You'll improve your chance of an E if you try one of the other tests as well.

To gain grade D, candidates *must* take one or more additional tests, choosing 'according to their needs and capabilities' from 'Basic Writing' or a 'Higher' test. In fact, it's a bit unrealistic to expect grade D on *one* additional test; other things being equal, more than one would be a better idea.

To gain grade C, you must take all four 'Basic' tests and at least one 'Higher' test. One 'Higher' test might just about get you a grade C, if you do all the papers very well. But it would be safer to take more than one.

To gain grade B, you'll need to take all the 'Basic' and all the 'Higher' tests. In theory, you *could* omit one or two 'Higher' tests (except 'Writing') and still get grade B, but it's pretty unlikely that your marks would then be enough to add up to grade B.

For grade A, similarly, it's *possible* to leave out one of the 'Higher' tests, as long as it isn't 'Writing', but the rest of your marks would have to be very high indeed to make up for the missing test.

You may well be wondering why, if it's safer to take more tests than the minimum, teachers don't simply enter all candidates for all the tests. The fact is that for some classes and for some schools, some tests are impractical.

'Higher Writing', for instance, demands a high degree of accuracy, requiring a great deal of class time for explanation and drills, and a great deal of homework. There's a risk that 'Writing' could end up dominating the course. One teacher used conscientiously to teach CSE groups to write in the perfect tense, because it was on the exam syllabus. Hours were spent learning, repeating, revising, drilling and correcting the perfect tense! Hours that gobbled up the time needed for the other skills. And *still* the students wrote it wrongly! (It can be a tricky concept, the perfect tense.) The year the teacher cut it out, grades soared: any marks lost in 'Writing' were more than compensated for by better 'Listening', 'Speaking' and 'Reading' scores.

'Higher Speaking' also requires much practice. In class, pupils must work sensibly in pairs without wasting time in idle chatter, or must listen and learn attentively as the teacher practises with one pupil. It's excellent when the group is small, well motivated and has plenty of time. But with a large and boisterous class following a crash course it could be a waste of good learning time.

Listening practice is expensive in terms of resources. It's perfect if your school has a foreign assistant, an annual exchange scheme and a video and tape-recorder in each languages room. Not so good if the school's only audible recorder is shared between three teachers.

Your school may decide not to enter your class for a test which you want to take. Perhaps, for instance, your group is not taking 'Higher Speaking', but you think you could cope because you're getting conversation lessons from the Swiss lady down the road. Discuss it with your teacher, and if necessary involve your parents and the Head, before entries are finalised in the spring term of the fifth year.

SECTION 2

Preparing for the exam

REVISING: HOW TO MAKE THE BEST USE OF YOUR TIME

Suppose you've just drawn your savings from the bank: a hundred £1 notes and two £50 notes. You're just counting them in the street, when a breeze blows them to the ground. What do you do? Grab as many as you can, starting with the nearest one? Or stand back long enough to spy your big notes, and go for those first? You can either scrabble around in a panic, find a few, lose a few, hope for the best, *or* you can make sure of the valuable ones, stow them safely, and then see what else you can pick up before the wind blows them all away.

Your time between now and the exams is like those notes. You know how much you have to start with, but suppose some is blown away? All that endless time which stretches before you will be nibbled away by homework, Saturday jobs, discos, visits to grandma, or even illness, tensions at home, or the love of your life. There will be times when you're too tired to revise, periods when you can't be bothered, and evenings when the three hours revision you'd planned turns out to be half an hour, and you decide it isn't worth getting the books out. So be safe: make sure you grasp what's most valuable first, and pick up the rest later if there's time.

Spread yourself evenly between all your subjects: better to get eight middling grades than one grade A and seven very low grades. And for each subject it's better to be *fairly* ready for *all* the questions, than brilliant at one part of one paper and useless at the rest. It's astonishing how many candidates insist that one very good answer will somehow make up for a lot of poor ones. But the mark scheme just won't allow it: if you're taking four tests for 25% each, there's no way you can score *more* than 25% for any one of them, however stunning your script is.

Revising modern languages

The tests of listening, reading, speaking and writing all carry equal marks, so you need to develop each of these skills evenly. Each test will sample widely from the list of situations and topics on page 16, so you need to be familiar with them all. This is how.

Phase 1: Learn at school. If you do your classwork and homework adequately, and nothing more, you'll meet the whole syllabus, though you won't necessarily *know* it or be able to *use* it. Cross your fingers, hope for good luck, and you'll get a grade, but not the best that you're capable of. So, for a higher grade, move on to Phase 2.

Phase 2: Learn from this book, to consolidate the grounding given in school. Then, with any time you've got left, go on to Phase 3.

Phase 3: Learn from other sources. Then you're no longer relying on the teacher (Phase 1) or these pages (Phase 2), but you are fully in control of your own mastery of the subject. And that's what the highest grades are for.

Phase 1: Learn at school

Listening

The more the better:
listening to a variety of voices/ accents/speeds, from tapes/films/ visitors;
hearing your teacher using the language as much as possible; hearing natural, unscripted speech, even if there are parts which you don't understand.

Of doubtful value:
hearing the language spoken only very . . . slowly . . . with . . . unnatural . . . gaps . . . between . . . the . . . words;
only hearing specially written texts which protect you from exposure to unfamiliar words.

Reading

The more the better:
any reading matter, preferably written *by* and *for* native speakers (not by British teachers for British learners).

Of doubtful value:
translating complete passages into perfect English.

Speaking

The more the better:
talking about yourself (your interests, environment, future plans and so on);
asking other people about themselves;
learning to cope on a trip abroad.

Of doubtful value:
if the *only* speaking you do is reading aloud from a book, and reading out the answers to exercises in your book (especially exercises in which everybody is expected to produce the same answer).

Writing

The more the better:
writing tasks of the kind required by your exam Group (see page 14);
exercises which help you perform these tasks correctly.

Of doubtful value:
practising grammatical rules which you are unlikely to need in your speaking or writing.

Your own work

Let's assume that your school is giving you a balanced diet of useful practice. That's good, but it's not enough: *you've got to do your own work*. If the school could do it all for you, there'd be no need for exams, just grades of teacher: Miss X is a grade B teacher, so all her class gets grade B! Of course, if you've read as far as here in this book, you probably *are* prepared to work, so let's move on to Phase 2.

Phase 2: Learn from this book

1 Getting ready

Turn to the list of setting and topics on page 16 and copy each item on to the top of a separate sheet of paper or file card. Separate sheets are better than a notebook, because you don't know how much space you'll need under each heading.

Even if your zeal runs out at this stage, you are at least aware of what to notice particularly in class.

2 Speaking

Anything you learn to *say* you are automatically learning to *understand* for 'Reading' and 'Listening', and with a little extra effort you can learn to *spell* the same phrases for 'Writing'.

In the 'Speaking' sections, which begin on page 28 for French and page 47 for German, you'll find key sentences for each setting and topic on the list. The sections don't − couldn't possibly − include *everything* you might want to say. The sentences have been carefully chosen to cover: *all the settings and topics*, so that whatever subjects crop up in the exam, you'll be prepared; *all the vocabulary areas*, so that you've got the words to talk about the subjects which crop up; *the most useful sentence patterns*, so that you can combine the words you know. All the sentences have words enclosed in brackets, which can be replaced by other words to make new sentences which are as good as the originals. If you were an 'O' level candidate, it would be advisable to learn all the sentences by heart, however tedious the task. But you're part of the new, thinking, GCSE generation. What you need to do, is replace all the words in brackets with words *of your own*. Your new sentences will be much more memorable than the originals, just because they're yours.

So turn to the 'Role-play' section for your language and start thinking of substitutes for all the words in brackets. You'll learn it best if you copy the English introductions and your French/German sentences on to the headed paper or card. If you can't think of a bracket-filler for the moment, leave a blank space in the sentence, and bear it in mind. Sooner or later, during school work or revision, you'll probably come across something. Get your teacher's help as a second-to-last resort, and use a dictionary only as a very last resort. Make a start on *all* the role-play sentences − better to hurry through all the settings than to learn only the first one thoroughly.

The 'Conversation' section is slightly different, because not all its sentences will apply to you. For instance, if you have no pets at home, you can leave out the sentence on pets. If you're totally uninterested in sport, you don't have to talk about sporting activities. On the other hand, if you *are* a pet owner or a sports fanatic you must find out the relevant vocabulary to replace the words in the brackets.

3 Grammar

The numbers in brackets in the 'Speaking' sections refer to units in the 'Grammar' sections (French, page 33; German, page 51). The grammar in this book deals *only* with rules needed for those 'Speaking' sentences. So they're all essential if you're to make your own sentences for 'Speaking'. The explanations are very brief. They don't include *all* the grammar you need for grade A, but they do show where to begin and what are the most important facts. The words in capitals are the headings which will most probably give you more details in your school text-book grammar summary.

If you're taking 'Higher Speaking' or 'Basic Writing', you need to know the 'Grammar' section well if you are to avoid making what are considered elementary errors. For 'Higher Writing', you will certainly need to find out more grammar.

4 Listening and reading
Read the tips and short cuts to understanding (French, page 39; German, page 57). They don't always work, because languages aren't codes, but they will help.

5 Writing
You will need to know the formulae for beginning and ending letters (French, page 45; German, page 66). They are set out with the English in one column, French/German in the other, so that you can cover the French/German and test yourself from the English. If you know alternative phrases with the same meaning, that's fine. The important thing is that you know *some* way of rendering all those phrases.

6 Learning
If you've worked through **1-5**, you're familiar with what you need to know. Now learn it.

Role-play:
- **(a)** cover the French/German and see if you can remember it from the English introduction;
- **(b)** try to think of a further alternative to the word or phrase in the box.

Conversation:
practise saying your sentences about yourself. Aloud.

Reading and listening:
do the exercises in these sections, if you didn't have time before.

Writing letters:
test yourself by covering the French/German and trying to write the formulae with perfect spelling. If you can't be bothered to learn them accurately, you're throwing marks away before you start.

Phase 3: Learn from other sources

1 Use your school text-books
Keep handy a notebook or paper divided into two columns. When you're working from your text-book, note down words and phrases which you might not need to say or write yourself, but which you must *understand* when you hear or see them, such as phrases which a shop-assistant might use to you, or street signs. Add the English in the right-hand column. Include words which are rare in English but common

in French/German. For instance, you probably rarely think about Epiphany, but in France the *Fête des Rois*, which is the same festival, is a special family occasion. It is unlikely that 'Shrovetide' is constantly on your lips, but in German it's *Fasching*, so important a festival that it's practically an industry. Don't bother to write down words whose meaning is obvious, or already known to you. In odd moments, test yourself by covering up the English and seeing if you remember the meanings.

At the same time, look out for words and phrases to add to your 'Speaking' lists (point **2** above). If they are words which don't concern everybody, the teacher may not stress them. But if they apply to *you*, you should make a note of them. For instance, if you're interested in sport, scour your course-book for words and phrases which you might want to use ('I fell on the ski slope and broke my leg', 'I scored the winning goal'). Collect phrases which echo your feelings or opinions on any of the 'Conversation' topics, adapting them if necessary to yourself. Try an example. (Answers on page 28.)

Example in French
Read this extract from a text-book:

Vous habitez où … ?

Le rêve du Français moyen est de posséder une maison, sa propre maison, surtout avec un petit jardin. A la campagne on habite souvent dans des maisons individuelles, mais dans les villes et en banlieue c'est autre chose. Très peu de familles ont une maison particulière. Presque tout le monde habite un appartement. Ces appartements se trouvent d'habitude dans des immeubles ou même dans de grandes tours.

Now suppose you live in a block of flats in the suburbs, but you'd like to have your own house with a little garden in the country. Copy or adapt phrases to add to your 'Conversation' notes on the topic of *home*.

. . . .
. . . .
. . . .

Example in German
Read this extract from a text-book:

> Dieter Lorsch ist Bademeister im
> Hallenbad Fechingen. Oft muß er
> am Wochenende arbeiten. Er
> braucht keinen Wagen. Er wohnt
> in der Stadtmitte und fährt mit
> der Linie 1 nach Fechingen. Ab
> und zu fährt er mit seinem
> Freund. Seine Arbeit ist nicht
> schwer, und er kann schwimmen
> so oft er will.

Now suppose you've got a weekend job in the city centre. You get there on the Number 1 bus. Your work isn't difficult. Copy or adapt phrases to add to your 'Conversation' notes on the topic of *work*.

. . . .
. . . .
. . . .

2 Other school resources
Who's using the school languages tapes overnight? You could try asking your teacher if you could borrow a cassette to play at home, if you have a player.

3 Native speakers or their writing
Make the most of any contacts you have. Profit from recordings, film strips, photos, videos, or trips provided by your school, and from holiday slides, old bus-tickets, posters, visitors and foreign food packets brought in by your teacher.

4 Yourself
Use your own initiative to adapt and expand the revision suggestions given above. The most successful students start by accepting guidance from those experienced in exam techniques, and end with a personalised set of study skills to suit their own weaknesses and strengths.

ANSWERS

French *habite un appartement – dans un immeuble – en banlieue – posséder ma propre maison – avec un petit jardin – à la campagne.*

German *am Wochenende arbeiten – in der Stadtmitte – fahre mit der Linie 1 – meine Arbeit ist nicht schwer.*

FRENCH SPEAKING: ROLE-PLAY

This section contains key sentences for each setting and topic. Replace the words in square brackets with words of your own (see page 24). The numbers which follow some of the French sentences refer to units in the 'Grammar' section.

Visiting

Introduce a friend or relation: *Voici [ma voisine Anne]*. (26) Wish someone well: *Bon [voyage]!* (21) Ask permission: *Est-ce que je peux [téléphoner à mes parents]?* (9, 26) Thank someone for a meal, a gift, their help, etc.: *Merci pour [le repas]. C'était [délicieux]*.

Sightseeing

Ask whether there is a place or facility near here: *Est-ce qu'il y a [un bureau de change] près d'ici?* Ask whether the tourist office has information, tickets, etc.: *Avez-vous [une liste d'hôtels]?* Ask what there is to do/ see in a place: *Qu'est-ce qu'il y a à faire/ voir [à Dieppe]?* (29) Ask if or when a place or service is open or closed: *(Quand) est-ce que [le bureau] est fermé/ ouvert?* Ask the way to a place: *Pour aller [au marché]?* (29) Ask if a place is near/far away: *[La plage], c'est près/ loin d'ici?*

Eating

Say which menu you want: *Je voudrais le menu [à prix fixe]*. (29) Ask for an explanation of menu terms: *[Le plat du jour], qu'est-ce que c'est?* Order/ Ask for more/ Ask if they have drinks, snacks, ice-creams: *Je voudrais/ Encore/ Avez-vous [un sandwich au jambon]*. (29) Ask what kind of . . . they have: *Qu'est-ce que vous avez comme [sandwichs]?*

Travelling

Find out if there is transport: *Est-ce qu'il y a un (autre) [car] pour . . .?* Find out when there is transport: *À quelle heure est-ce qu'il y a un [autobus] pour . . . ?* Ask about departure times: *À quelle heure part [le train*] *pour . . .?* (8) Ask about arrival times: *À quelle heure est-ce que* [*le ferry*] *arrive à . . .?* (2) Make a reservation: *Je voudrais réserver* [*une place*] *dans* [*le bateau*] *pour . . .* (1) Buy return/ single tickets, first/ second class: *Un* [*aller-simple*], [*première*] *classe, pour . . .* (21) Ask where your transport or departure point is: *Pour* [*la gare*], *c'est quel* [*arrêt d'autobus*]? (21) Check you've found the right vehicle: *C'est bien* [*le train*] *pour . . .?* Check you're going the right way: *Est-ce que* [*cet autobus*] *va à* [*la gare SNCF*]? (7, 22) Ask for facilities in the station: *Où est* [*le bureau de renseignements*]? (4) Say when you'll arrive/ leave: *Je vais arriver/ partir* [*le 3 août*]. (14, 27)

Driving

Ask for 2-star/ 4-star petrol by quantity or value: [*Le plein*] *de super/ d'ordinaire, s'il vous plaît.* Get parts of your car checked: *Vérifiez* [*l'eau*], *s'il vous plaît.* (17) Say what has broken down, and ask if the garage can help: [*Ma voiture*] *est en panne. Pouvez-vous* [*envoyer un mécanicien*]? (9, 26) Say where you are: *Je suis en panne* [*entre Avranches et Granville*].

Shopping

Find out whether shopping places are nearby: *Est-ce qu'il y a* [*une pâtisserie*] *près d'ici?* Ask where shops/ parts of shops are: *Où est* [*le rayon des disques*]? Say what food/ clothes/ souvenirs/ etc. you'd like to buy (or ask the price, or ask if they have any): *Je voudrais/ C'est combien/ Avez-vous* [*un kilo de pêches*]. (30) Say that you'd like to try/ see clothes/ etc.: *Je voudrais essayer/ voir* [*des T-shirts*]. (11) Say what quantity you want: *Je voudrais* [*un paquet de biscuits*]. (30) Say why you don't want to buy: *C'est trop* [*cher*].

Going out

Invite somebody somewhere: *Je vais* [*à un match de rugby*]. *Tu veux venir?* (7, 11) Find out what a friend wants to do: *Qu'est-ce que tu veux* [*voir*]? (11) Suggest a time and place to meet: *On se rencontre* [*à huit heures*] [*devant la piscine*]? (15) Say when you'll meet again: *Au revoir! À* [*samedi soir*]! (29) Ask when an event begins or ends: *À quelle heure est-ce que* [*le film*] *commence/ finit?* (3) Buy tickets and ask about price reductions: [*Deux places*]. *Est-ce qu'il y a des réductions pour* [*étudiants*]?

Post office, phone, bank

Find out where you can phone/ post letters/ change money: *Est-ce qu'il y a* [*une boîte aux lettres*] *près d'ici?* Ask about services and prices there:

Je voudrais	*envoyer une lettre en Angleterre*	. (11, 31)
C'est combien pour	*téléphoner d'ici à Londres*	? (1, 29)
Est-ce que je peux	*parler à M. Boileau*	?

Buy stamps: *Je voudrais un timbre à [1 F 60]*. (29)

Accommodation

Say what accommodation you'd like (or say you've reserved, or ask what they have available):

Je voudrais	*une chambre*		*[avec salle de bains]* . (28)
Avez-vous	*un emplacement*	*pour*	*[une caravane]* ?
J'ai réservé	*deux lits*	*pour*	*[trois nuits]*. (12)

Ask where things are in the camp/ hotel/ hostel: *Où est [ma clé]*? Ask where/ whether you can do something: *(Où) est-ce que je peux [laisser ma moto]*? (9) Ask about meal times: *[Le petit déjeuner], c'est à quelle heure?* Buy camping supplies: *Je voudrais [une boîte d'allumettes]*. Say what bedding/ transport/ equipment you'd like to hire: *Je voudrais louer [un sac de couchage]*. (11) Ask the price: *C'est combien par [personne]*? Find out what extras you have to pay for: *Est-ce que [le service] est compris?*

Illness

Say how you feel: *Je suis [fatigué]*. (4) *J'ai [chaud]*. (5) Say how long you've been hurting where: *J'ai mal [à la tête] depuis [deux jours]*. (5, 29) Say what you'd like to do about it: *Je voudrais [aller au lit]*. (11, 27) Ask a chemist for something for your complaint: *Je voudrais quelque chose pour le mal de [dents]*. Say what you need: *J'ai besoin [d'aspirine]*. (5)

Lost property

Say what you've lost/ left behind, where, and when: *J'ai perdu/ laissé [mon passeport] [dans le musée] [ce matin]*. (12) Describe the lost object: *C'est [un petit sac bleu] en [plastique]* . (25, 31)

Language

Say which languages you speak: *Je (ne) parle (pas) [français]*. (19) Say which languages you understand: *Je (ne) comprends (pas) [l'allemand]*. (10, 19) Ask somebody to repeat, write, spell, speak more slowly, etc.: *Voulez-vous [répéter], s'il vous plaît?* (11) Ask for translations: *Qu'est-ce que c'est en [français]?*

FRENCH SPEAKING: CONVERSATION

This section contains key sentences for use in French conversation. Make use of those which apply to you, by replacing the words in brackets with words of your own (see page 24). The numbers which follow some of the French sentences refer to units in the 'Grammar' section.

People

Name: *Je m'appelle* . . . (15) Family: *J'ai [deux soeurs], mais je n'ai pas de [frères].* (30) *[Mon grand frère] s'appelle* . . . (20, 26) Age: *[Il a]* . . . *ans.* (5) Pets: *[Nous avons] [un petit chien noir].* (5, 20, 25) Description: *J'ai les cheveux [très longs] et [blonds].* (20, 25) *Je suis [assez petit].* (4, 20) *[Ma soeur est] [intelligente]. [Elle est] plus [intelligente] que [moi].* (24)

Leisure

Sport: *Je (ne) suis (pas) très [sportif/ sportive].* (19, 21) *J'aime regarder [le football] [à la télé].* (27) *J'aime jouer [au rugby].* (29) *J'aime faire [du cheval].* (6) TV, radio, etc.: *Je regarde la télé/ J'écoute la radio/ Je vais au cinéma [tous les soirs].* (2, 23, 7) *J'aime [les vieux films].* (27) Music: *J'aime [le rock et le jazz].* (27) *J'ai [un magnétophone] et [beaucoup de cassettes].* (30) *Je joue [de la trompette] dans [un orchestre à vents].* (30) Hobbies: *J'aime [lire].* (1) *J'aime [la photographie].* (27) Going out: *Je sors [le samedi soir] avec [des copains].* (8, 27) *Je vais [au club] [pour jouer au billard].* (1, 29)

Home

Birth: *Je suis né à* . . . *en 19* . . . (13, 29) *Je suis [anglais].* (20) Address: *J'habite à* . . . *C'est [une petite ville] dans [le nord] de [l'Angleterre].* (20, 27) *Mon adresse/ numéro de téléphone est* . . . Local town: . . . *est une ville [industrielle].* (20, 25) *Il y a des [monuments historiques].* (20, 25) *Il n'y a pas de [bâtiments importants].* (19, 30) *Il y a [un vieux château].* (21) *Pour les gens sportifs il y a [une salle des sports].* (25) *Pour s'amuser, on va [à la maison des jeunes].* (7, 29) House/flat: *J'habite dans [un appartement assez moderne].* (25) *Nous avons [trois chambres]. Ma chambre est [jolie mais petite].* (20) *Dans ma chambre j'ai [mes disques et ma télé].* (26) Routine: *Je [me lève] à* . . . *heures.* (2, 15) *[Vendredi soir] nous [faisons les courses].* (6) Recent events (when and what you did): *[Hier soir] j'ai [vu un film formidable].* (12)

Weather, date, seasons

Date, day: *Aujourd'hui/ Mon anniversaire/ La fête nationale, c'est le [quatorze juillet]. Aujourd'hui, nous sommes [lundi].* (4) Weather:

Aujourd'hui il [fait beau]. (6) Past weather: *[Hier] il [faisait beau]*. (16)
Seasons: *Il [fait froid] [en hiver] [en Écosse]* . (31)

Holidays

In general: *Pendant les vacances nous allons [au bord de la mer]*. (2, 7,
29) *Nous passons [deux semaines] [sous une tente]*. (2) Activities: *À la
plage/ campagne, nous [faisons des piques-niques]*. (6) Future:

L'année prochaine		*je vais*		*aller [à Paris]*. (14, 20)
Cet été		*je voudrais*		*visiter [Rome]*. (22)
En hiver		*j'espère*		*faire [du ski]*. (31, 6)

Past: *L'année dernière/ Il y a . . . ans, je suis allé [à la montagne]*. (13)
J'ai [fait du camping]. (12) *Je me suis bien amusé*. (15) Trips abroad:
Je suis allé [une] fois [à l'étranger]. (13) *Je ne suis jamais allé [en
France]*. (13, 19) *J'ai vu/ visité [la tour Eiffel]*. (12) *J'ai fait le voyage
[en avion et par le train]*. (12, 31) *J'ai beaucoup aimé [la cuisine et les
plages]*. (12)

Work

School: *Mon collège est [grand] et [moderne]. Il est situé [à 2 km de
chez moi]*. (29) *J'y vais [à pied]*. (31) *C'est un collège mixte/ de garçons/
de filles*. (25) *Il y a [cinq cents] élèves. Nous avons [une piscine et deux
bibliothèques]. Les cours commencent à [huit heures] et finissent à
[cinq heures]*. (3) *Nous avons . . . semaines de vacances à [Nöel]*.
School work: *Au collège j'apprends [les maths]*. (10, 27) *Ma matière
préférée est [la physique], parce que c'est [intéressant]*. (27) *J'apprends
[le français] depuis . . . ans*. (10) *Je suis en [seconde]*. (28) Future
plans: *Je vais [passer des examens] et puis [quitter l'école]*. (27, 14)
Je voudrais être [mécanicien]. (14, 28) *J'espère travailler [dans un
garage]*. (14) Jobs in the family: *[Mon père] est [professeur]*. (26, 28)
[Ma mère] travaille [dans un hôpital]. (2) Part-time jobs: *[Le dimanche]
je travaille [dans un café]*. (27, 2) *Je gagne [une livre] par [heure]*. (2)
J'achète [des disques et des vêtements]. (2) Dreams: *Je fais des écono-
mies pour acheter [une motocyclette]*. (1) *Si j'étais riche, [j'achèterais
une voiture de sport]*. (18)

Opinions

Likes/dislikes concerning, e.g. food, sports, programmes, school subjects:

J'aime		*les cerises*		. (2, 27)
J'adore		*les petits pois*		.
Je déteste		*les vieux films*		.
Je n'aime pas		*la gymnastique*		.
Je préfère		*la biologie*		.

Preferences: *Mon [sport] préféré est [la pêche]*. (25, 27) Opinions: *Je
trouve ça [intéressant]*.

32

FRENCH GRAMMAR

This section deals with basic grammar rules which crop up in sentences in the 'Speaking' sections (see page 24).

Examples

1

J'aime regarder le sport à la télé.
En hiver, j'espère faire du ski.
Je vais arriver jeudi à midi.
Je voudrais réserver une place.
Pour aller au musée, s'il vous plaît?

2

J'habite dans un appartement.
Ma mère travaille dans un hôpital.
Je gagne deux livres par heure.
Nous passons deux semaines sous une tente.
Quand est-ce que le ferry arrive?

3

À quelle heure est-ce que le spectacle finit?
Les cours finissent à quatre heures.

4

Je suis assez petit.
Où est le bureau?
Où sont les toilettes?
Aujourd'hui nous sommes lundi.

5

Mon frère a dix ans.
Nous avons un petit chien noir.
Avez-vous une liste d'hôtels?
J'ai seize ans.
J'ai chaud/ froid/ soif/ faim.
J'ai besoin d'aspirine.

Grammar notes

These **er** and **re** endings, which sometimes translate as 'to', are INFINITIVES. They are used when you say what you *like* to do, *hope* to do, are *going* to do, *would like* to do, and after **pour**. Some infinitives end in **ir**.

These sentences are about something happening *regularly* or *now*, so they are in the PRESENT TENSE. The present ends in **e** with *I, he, she* or *it*, and **ons** with *we*, for regular verbs with **er** infinitives.

These PRESENT TENSE endings are different, because they are from **finir**, an **ir** verb.

Units **4–11** contain IRREGULAR VERBS, those whose endings don't follow a pattern. These examples are from **être** (to be).

These sentences contain parts of **avoir** (to have).

In these phrases, French uses **avoir** where English uses 'to be'.

6

Vendredi soir nous **faisons** *les courses.*
Je **fais** *du sport chaque jour.*
J'aime **faire** *du cheval.*
Il **fait** *froid en hiver en Écosse.*

The verb **faire** (to do, to make) is also used in phrases about leisure and the weather.

7

Je **vais** *au cinéma de temps en temps.*
Pendant les vacances nous **allons** *au bord de la mer.*
Est-ce que cet autobus **va** *à la gare SNCF?*

These sentences contain parts of **aller** (to go).

8

À quelle heure **part** *le train?*
Je **sors** *le samedi soir.*

The verbs **partir** (to leave) and **sortir** (to go out) have similar endings.

9

Pouvez-vous *envoyer un mécanicien?*
Où est-ce que je **peux** *laisser ma moto?*

The verb **pouvoir** (to be able, can) is followed by an infinitive showing what somebody can do.

10

*J'***apprends** *le français depuis cinq ans.*
Je ne **comprends** *pas.*

The verbs **apprendre** (to learn) and **comprendre** (to understand) have the same endings as **prendre** (to take).

11

Je **voudrais** *voir des T-shirts.*
Je **voudrais** *envoyer une lettre en Angleterre.*
Tu **veux** *venir?*

An infinitive after **vouloir** (to want) shows what somebody wants to do. *Je voudrais* (I would like) is the conditional of *vouloir*.

Voulez-vous *répéter, s'il vous plaît?*

'Voulez-vous . . .?' is a polite way of asking, 'Would you . . .?'

12

J'ai *réservé deux lits.*
J'ai *visité la tour Eiffel.*
J'ai *beaucoup aimé les plages.*
J'ai *perdu mon passeport.*
J'ai *fait du camping.*
*Hier soir j'*ai vu *un film formidable.*

These sentences about events in the past are in the PERFECT TENSE, formed from part of **avoir** with a past participle, often ending in **é** (**er** verbs) or **u** (**re** verbs). Some are irregular, e.g. *fait, vu.*

13

Je suis né(e) *à Cardiff.*
Je suis allé(e) *à l'étranger une fois.*

A few verbs form the PERFECT TENSE by using part of **être** instead of **avoir**. Their past participles add **e** if the subject is feminine.

14

Je vais passer *des examens et puis quitter l'école.*
Cet été je voudrais visiter *mon correspondant.*
*En hiver j'*espère faire *du ski.*

These sentences, about future intentions and hopes, use **je vais/ je voudrais/ j'espère** with an infinitive. The FUTURE TENSE could be used instead: *Je* passerai *des examens . . .*, etc.

15

Je me lève *à sept heures.*
Je m'appelle . . .
Mon grand frère s'appelle *David.*
On se rencontre *à huit heures?*
Pour s'amuser *on va à la maison des jeunes.*
Je me suis *bien amusé.*

The verbs in these sentences contain **me, m', se, s'**. They are REFLEXIVE VERBS.

In the perfect, reflexives take **être**.

16

Hier il faisait *froid.*
*C'*était *délicieux!*

These verbs, showing what *was happening* or what *used to happen*, are in the IMPERFECT TENSE.

17

Vérifiez l'eau, s'il vous plaît.

This **ez** ending is an IMPERATIVE, giving a command. Other examples: *Tournez à gauche. Continuez tout droit.*

18

*Si j'étais riche, j'achèterais une
voiture de sport.*
Je voudrais voir des T-shirts.

These verbs, which mean 'I
would . . .', are in the CON-
DITIONAL TENSE.

19

Je ne parle pas français.
Je n'aime pas ça.
Je n'ai pas de frères.
Je ne suis pas sportif.
*Il n'y a pas de bâtiments impor-
tants en ville.*
Je ne suis jamais allé en France.

These are NEGATIVE sentences;
in English they would need 'not'
or 'never'. Notice that the negative words go either side of a
verb.

20

Je suis assez petit.
Je suis anglais.
Mon grand frère s'appelle David.
Nous avons un petit chien noir.
Mon sport préféré est la pêche.
Ma soeur est intelligente.
Ma chambre est jolie mais petite.
*L'année prochaine je vais aller à
Paris.*
J'ai les cheveux longs et blonds.
*En ville il y a des monuments
historiques.*
*Il n'y a pas de bâtiments impor-
tants.*

The words in bold print are
ADJECTIVES. The first two
would need an extra e (*petite*,
anglaise) if the speaker were
female.
These adjectives have an added e
because *soeur, chambre* and
année are FEMININE.

These adjectives end in s because
cheveux, monuments and *bâtiments* are PLURAL. (Adding the
e and s is called AGREEMENT
OF ADJECTIVES.)

21

Je ne suis pas sportif.
Je suis sportive.
*Deux aller-simple première classe
pour Paris, s'il vous plaît.*
*L'année dernière nous sommes
allés à la montagne.*
Bon voyage! Bonnes vacances!
À quelle heure part le train?
Pour la gare, c'est quel arrêt?
Il y a un vieux château en ville.
J'ai perdu une vieille valise.

These IRREGULAR ADJEC-
TIVES make other changes,
besides adding e, when describing something or somebody
FEMININE, e.g.
f → ve: *sportif/sportive*
ier → ière: *premier/première*
             dernier/ dernière
bon → bonne
quel → quelle
vieux → vieille

22

J'ai perdu mon passeport **ce** *matin.*
Cet *été je voudrais visiter mon correspondant.*
Est-ce que **cet** *autobus va à la gare SNCF?*

Ce (this) is IRREGULAR. It becomes **cet** before a vowel and **cette** before a feminine word.

23

Je regarde la télé **tous** *les soirs.*

Tout (all) also IRREGULAR, is **tous** in the plural.

24

Ma soeur est **plus** *intelligente* **que** *moi.*

Plus *intelligente* **que** means '*more* intelligent *than*' or 'clever*er than*'. (This is COMPARISON OF ADJECTIVES.)

25

Il n'y a pas de bâtiments **impor-tants** *en ville.*
J'habite dans un appartement assez **moderne.**
C'est un collège **mixte.**
J'ai les cheveux **longs** *et* **blonds.**
Pour les gens **sportifs** *il y a une salle des sports.*
C'est un **petit** *sac* **bleu** *en plasti-que.*
C'est une **vieille** *valise* **rouge.**
Leeds est une **grande** *ville* **indus-trielle.**

Notice the POSITION OF AD-JECTIVES. Most adjectives *follow* the noun they describe.

A few, like **petit, grand, vieux,** come *before* the noun they describe.

26

Voici **ma** *voisine Anne.*
Mon *grand frère s'appelle David.*
Est-ce que je peux téléphoner à **mes** *parents?*
Ma *voiture est en panne.*
Dans **ma** *chambre j'ai* **mes** *disques et* **ma** *télé.*

'My' is **ma** before someone or something feminine, **mon** before something or someone masculine, and **mes** before a plural. The rules for the other POSSESSIVES (words for 'your', 'his', 'her', etc.) are similar.

27

J'aime les vieux films.
J'aime regarder le sport à la télé.
Mon sport préféré est la pêche.
Au collège j'apprends les maths.
C'est une ville dans le nord de l'Angleterre.
Je vais quitter l'école à seize ans.
Je suis allé à l'étranger une fois.
Je voudrais aller au lit.
Le *dimanche, je travaille dans un café.*
Je vais partir le 3 août.

28

Je voudrais une chambre avec salle de bains.
Je suis en seconde.
Je voudrais être mécanicien.

29

C'est combien pour téléphoner à Londres?
Je vais arriver jeudi à midi.
Pour aller au marché?
J'ai mal à la tête et aux dents.
Le collège est à deux kilomètres.
Je voudrais un timbre à 1F60.
Encore un sandwich au jambon!
Avez-vous des glaces à la fraise?
J'aime jouer au rugby.
Je suis né à Londres en Angleterre.

À samedi soir!

Le, la, l' and **les** (the DEFINITE ARTICLES) are often used in French where we would leave out 'the' in English; for instance, when naming likes, dislikes, school subjects and countries, and in the phrases: *à* l'*école, à* l'*étranger,* **au** *lit, à* **la** *maison, à* **la** *télé, à* **la** *radio.*
They can mean 'every' with days of the week or 'on the' with dates.

Sometimes French omits a word for 'a' or 'the' (the **ARTICLES**) where English would use one, e.g. after **en, avec, sans** and before jobs and professions.

Units **29–31** are about the PREPOSITIONS **à**, **de** and **en**. **À** generally means 'to' or 'at'.
À with **le** or **les** is shortened to **au** or **aux**.
À is used in expressions of distance, price, and flavour, and after **jouer** when it refers to playing games (not instruments).

'In' is translated as **à** before towns and in *à la compagne*, **en** before names of countries and in **en** *ville*.
À with a day or time means 'See you . . .'.

30

J'ai beaucoup **de** *cassettes.*	**De** (or **d'**) often means 'of' or
Je voudrais un kilo **de** *pêches.*	'from', and is found in phrases
Je voudrais un paquet **de** *biscuits.*	giving the quantity *of* something.
Avez-vous **des** *posters?*	**Du** (short for *de le*), **de la, de l'**
J'aime faire **du** *cheval.*	and **des** (short for *de les*) can
Je fais **du** *sport chaque jour.*	also mean 'some' or 'any'. Also
Je joue **de la** *trompette.*	used with **faire** and leisure activi-
	ties, and **jouer** with instruments.
Je n'ai pas **de** *frères.*	**De** is the word for 'any' when
Il n'y a pas **de** *bâtiments impor-*	there aren't any.
tants en ville.	

31

En *hiver j'espère faire du ski.*	**En** has many meanings, e.g. 'in'
Je voudrais envoyer une carte	with seasons (except **au** *prin-*
postale **en** *Angleterre.*	*temps*); 'in', 'at' or 'to' before
J'ai fait le voyage **en** *avion et par*	names of most countries; 'by' or
le train.	'on' with transport (except **par**
J'ai perdu une valise **en** *cuir.*	*le train* and à *pied*); 'made of'
	with a type of material.

FRENCH: LISTENING AND READING

This section suggests short cuts and ideas for you to think about and try to add to yourself. The answers to the quizzes are on page 44.

Listening: French-to-English sound patterns

'They speak so fast, I can't make out a word,' learners sigh when first exposed to authentic French speech. If they can hear it again and *read* what they hear at the same time, they are surprised at how much was in fact familiar. The thousands of words which *look* the same in French and English, or nearly, don't *sound* the same, so you need ways of hearing pattern and meaning in the sounds. Perhaps you've known toddlers with their own pattern of pronunciation. If a child shows you his toy snake and tells you it's a 'nake', you'll understand when he says there's a 'nail' or a 'lide' in the garden. You can use similar decoding skills to understand a language.

Quiz 1

The words overleaf look almost identical in both languages. Think about their pronunciation in French (or get someone to remind you) and notice which English sound corresponds to the letters in bold print.

Find at least two more examples of each French-to-English sound pattern in the bracketed list. To start you off: the letters **au** make the same sound in both *sauce* and *cause* in French. They make the same sound in both words in English too, but it's a different sound, a sort of 'aw'. Now look in the list for French words where the **au** also makes the sound 'aw' in English, and fill in the spaces. Some of the words in the list could go in more than one group.

Vowels

au	sauce, cause,	− − − − − −,	− − − − − −
è	scène, nièce,	− − − − − −,	− − − − −
i, y	pipe, style,	− − − − − −,	− − − − −
oi, oy	poison, royal,	− − − − − −,	− − − − −
ou	cousin, double,	− − − − − −,	− − − − −
en	accent, dense,	− − − − − −,	− − − − −
in	masculin, incident,	− − − − − −,	− − − − − −

Consonants

ch	chèque, chaîne,	− − − − − −,	− − − − −
g, j	agent, pyjama,	− − − − − −,	− − − − −
qu	liquide, question,	− − − − − −,	− − − − −
th	théâtre, mathématiques,	− − − − − −,	− − − − − −
d	grand-parent, second,	− − − − − −,	− − − − −
h	halte, hôtel,	− − − − − −,	− − − − −
l	détail, gorille,	− − − − − −,	− − − − −
t	fruit, transport,	− − − − − −,	− − − − −

automne	couple	hygiène	pastille	record
blond	danger	insecte	pause	secret
branche	fréquent	intention	pigeon	signe
cathédrale	guide	loyal	prince	tente
charme	hamster	méthode	queue	toilette
concert	hélicoptère	mètre	rail	trouble

Reading: French-to-English sight patterns

Reading French may be easier than listening, since so many words look identical or differ only because of an accent (*supplément, différence*), or an extra e (*tente, sûr*), or an extra **u** (*couleur, mouvement*), or **qu** for 'c' (*indiquer, musique*), or some other small difference (*géographie, caractère*).

Below there are some other similarities between French and English. They work often enough to make the meanings of many words clear.

Quiz 2

Read through the examples, then find another example of each pattern from the list overleaf. Some words will fit in more than one group.

French prefix	English	Examples
dé	dis	*déguiser, décourager,* — — — — —
dé	de, un	*décaféiné, défaire,* — — — — —
éc	sc, esc	*école, écarlate,* — — — — —
ép	sp	*épeler, épice,* — — — — —
esp	sp	*espace, esprit* (spirit), — — — — —
ét	st, est	*étranger, étudiant,* — — — — —
im, in	un, not, im	*inconnu* (unknown), *imprévu* (unforeseen), — — — — —
pré	fore	*prévu* (foreseen), *prédire* (foretell), — — — —
re	re, again	*recommencer, rentrer,* — — — — —
sou, sous	sub, under	*souterrain* (underground), *sous-vêtements,* — — — — —

French suffix	English	Examples
ant	ing	*charmant, intéressant,* — — — — —
é	ed	*habillé* (dressed), *fatigué,* — — — — —
té	ty	*beauté, cité,* — — — — —
eur	er, or	*directeur, employeur,* — — — — —
eur	ness	*hauteur* (highness, height), *douceur* (sweetness), — — — — —
aine	about . . .	*dixaine, cinquantaine,* — — — — —
aire	ary	*dictionnaire, secrétaire,* — — — — —
oire	ory	*réfectoire, gloire,* — — — — —
ment	ly	*immédiatement, automatiquement,* — — — —
er	tree	*oranger, poirier,* — — — — —
eux	ous	*précieux, merveilleux,* — — — — —
ir	ish	*punir, abolir,* — — — — —
er, ier	job	*glacier* (ice-cream maker), *pâtissier,* — — — —

41

French	English	Examples
ê, î, ô, û	es, is, os, us	*coûter* (to cost), *intérêt*, *île*, – – – – –

blancheur	*douzaine*	*finir*	*nécessaire*
boucher	*écran*	*forêt*	*pommier*
curieux	*éponge*	*impoli*	*prénom*
découvrir	*Espagne*	*laboratoire*	*retrouver*
déformé	*état*	*lentement*	*situé*
difficulté	*fatigant*	*mineur*	*sous-marin*

Quiz 3

Now look through these French words, and find the matching English word from the list underneath. All of them follow the patterns above. Some will need a lot more thought than others.

août	– – – – –	*épouse*	– – – – –
bête	– – – – –	*espion*	– – – – –
bonheur	– – – – –	*établir*	– – – – –
conducteur	– – – – –	*étouffer*	– – – – –
débarquer	– – – – –	*incroyable*	– – – – –
dégeler	– – – – –	*inquiet*	– – – – –
dégoûtant	– – – – –	*prévision*	– – – – –
délier	– – – – –	*renouveler*	– – – – –
dépanneuse	– – – – –	*soucoupe*	– – – – –
déplaire	– – – – –	*souligner*	– – – – –
désapprouver	– – – – –	*sous-sol*	– – – – –
échafaudage	– – – – –	*vacancier*	– – – – –

August	disembark	happiness	stifle
basement	disgusting	holidaymaker	unbelievable
beast	displease	renew	underline
breakdown lorry	driver	saucer	untie
defrost	establish	scaffolding	wife
disapprove	forecast	spy	worried

Reading: False friends

Occasionally, words *look* similar in French and English, but *don't* have the same meanings.

Quiz 4

Fit each of the words in the list below to its usual meaning. The first one is done for you.

False meaning	Usual meaning	French word
big	wide	*large*
smell	flavour	— — — — —
sleeping quarters	telephone kiosk	— — — — —
memorial	important building	— — — — —
place to stay in town	town hall	— — — — —
finished	full up, no vacancies	— — — — —
place to go for walk	a walk or trip	— — — — —
money for old people	charges for accommodation	— — — — —
where actors stand	course of instruction	— — — — —
letters	place to change bus/ train	— — — — —
guide on a tour	letters, mail	— — — — —
jetty (for boats)	platform (for trains)	— — — — —
remedy for illness	doctor	— — — — —
coins and bank notes	change	— — — — —
where books are loaned	bookshop	— — — — —
a better job	a special offer	— — — — —
to help	to be present	— — — — —
snapshot	photographer	— — — — —
underground hole	cellar	— — — — —
opportunity	good luck	— — — — —

assister	correspondance	médecin	photographe
cabine	courrier	monnaie	promenade
cave	hôtel de ville	monument	promotion
chance	large	parfum	quai
complet	librairie	pension	stage

Quiz 5

More deceptive appearances. Do you know the meanings of the words in bold type?

Sign in shop: **LOCATION** DE VOITURES
Road sign: **SENS** UNIQUE

Sign at car park entrance: INTERDIT AUX **CARS**
Instruction on vending machine: **Introduisez** 2 **pièces** de 1 F.
Notice in petrol station: **ESSENCE**, LAVAGE, HUILE
Maman, je te **présente** *mon ami Jules.*
Je suis en retard à cause de la *circulation.*
C'est le **conducteur** *qui a causé l'accident.*
J'ai rangé mes **affaires** *dans ma valise.*

ANSWERS

Quiz 1

Vowels			Consonants	
au	*automne, pause*		*ch*	*charme, branche*
è	*hygiène, mètre*		*g, j*	*danger, pigeon*
i, y	*signe, guide*		*qu*	*fréquent, queue*
oi, oy	*toilette, loyal*		*th*	*cathédrale, méthode*
ou	*trouble, couple*		*d*	*record, blond*
en	*tente, intention*		*h*	*hélicoptère, hamster*
in	*prince, insecte*		*l*	*rail, pastille*
			t	*secret, concert*

Quiz 2

dé	dis	*découvrir*	*té*	ty	*difficulté*
dé	de	*déformé*	*eur*	er, or	*mineur*
éc	sc	*écran*	*eur*	ness	*blancheur*
ép	sp	*éponge*	*aine*	about . . .	*douzaine*
esp	sp	*Espagne*	*aire*	ary	*nécessaire*
ét	st	*état*	*oire*	ory	*laboratoire*
im	not	*impoli*	*ment*	ly	*lentement*
pré	fore	*prénom*	*er*	tree	*pommier*
re	again	*retrouver*	*eux*	ous	*curieux*
sou	sub	*sous-marin*	*ir*	ish	*finir*
ant	ing	*fatigant*	*er*	job	*boucher*
é	ed	*situé*	*ê*	es	*forêt*

Quiz 3

août: August; *bête:* beast; *bonheur:* happiness; *conducteur:* driver; *débarquer:* disembark; *dégeler:* defrost; *dégoûtant:* disgusting; *délier:* untie; *dépanneuse:* breakdown lorry; *déplaire:* displease; *désapprouver:* disapprove; *échafaudage:* scaffolding; *épouse:* wife; *espion:* spy; *établir:* establish; *étouffer:* stifle; *incroyable:* unbelievable; *inquiet:* worried; *prévision:* forecast; *renouveler:* renew; *soucoupe:* saucer; *souligner:* underline; *sous-sol:* basement; *vacancier:* holidaymaker.

Quiz 4

flavour: **parfum**; telephone kiosk: **cabine**; important building: **monument**; town hall: **hôtel de ville**; full up, no vacancies: **complet**; a walk or trip: **promenade**; charges for accommodation: **pension**; course of instruction: **stage**; place to change bus/ train: **correspondance**; letters, mail: **courrier**; platform: **quai**; doctor: **médecin**; change: **monnaie**; bookshop: **librairie**; a special offer: **promotion**; to be present: **assister**; photographer: **photographe**; cellar: **cave**; good luck: **chance**.

Quiz 5

location: hire; **sens:** way; **cars:** coaches; **introduisez:** insert; **pièces:** coins; **essence:** petrol; **présente:** introduce; **circulation:** traffic; **conducteur:** driver; **affaires:** things, possessions.

FRENCH: WRITING LETTERS

Learn all these phrases and test yourself by covering the French words and working from the English (see page 25).

Informal letters

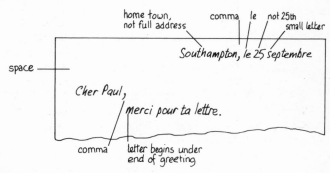

Beginning
Cher ...	Dear (writing to a boy) ...
Chère ...	Dear (writing to a girl) ...
Je te remercie de ta lettre.	Thanks for your letter.

Ending
Je dois te quitter maintenant.	I've got to go now.
Ecris-moi bientôt.	Write to me soon.
Amitiés	Best wishes
Ton ami	Your friend (if you're a boy)
Ton amie	Your friend (if you're a girl)

Formal letters

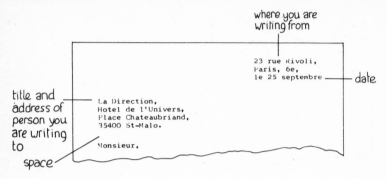

where you are writing from

23 rue Rivoli,
Paris, 6e,
le 25 septembre — date

title and address of person you are writing to

La Direction,
Hotel de l'Univers,
Place Chateaubriand,
35400 St-Malo.

Monsieur,

space

Beginning
Monsieur,
Madame,
Je vous remercie de votre lettre
du 5 avril.

Dear Sir,
Dear Madam,
Thank you for your letter of
5 April.

Middle
J'écris pour vous ⎡ *demander* ⎤
⎢ *dire* ⎥
Voulez-vous bien me ⎢ *faire savoir* ⎥
m' ⎣ *envoyer* ⎦

I'm writing to ⎡ ask ⎤ you
⎢ tell ⎥
Would you kindly ⎢ inform ⎥ me
⎣ send ⎦

Ending
The ending formula is not easy to learn. The only thing to do is persevere.

Veuillez agréer, Monsieur/
Madame, l'expression de mes
sentiments distingués.

Yours sincerely,

GERMAN SPEAKING: ROLE-PLAY

This section contains key sentences for each setting and topic. Replace the words in square brackets with words of your own (see page 24). The numbers which follow some of the German sentences refer to units in the 'Grammar' section.

Visiting

Introduce a friend or relation: *Hier ist [meine Freundin Paula]*. (12) Wish someone well: *Guten [Appetit]*! (18) Ask permission: *Darf ich [meine Eltern anrufen]*? (5) Thank someone: *Danke vielmals. Das ist sehr [nett]*.

Sightseeing

Ask whether/ where there is a place or facility near here: *Gibt es hier in der Nähe [ein Freibad]*? (11, 12) Ask whether the tourist office has information, tickets, etc.: *Haben Sie [einen Stadtplan]*? (11) Ask what there is to see/ do in a place: *Was gibt es [heute abend] in [der Stadt] zu sehen/ tun*? (14) Ask if or when a place is open/ closed: *(Wann) ist [die Sparkasse] geöffnet/ geschlossen*? Ask whether you can visit local sights: *Kann ich [das Rathaus] besichtigen*? (5, 12) Ask the way to a place: *Wie komme ich am besten [zur Kirche]*? (15)

Eating

Ask for an explanation of menu terms: *Was ist [die Tagessuppe]*? Order/ Ask for more/ Ask if they have food and drinks: *Ich nehme/ Noch/ Haben Sie [eine Tasse Kaffee]*. (4, 23) Ask what kind of . . . they have: *Was für [Eis] haben Sie*? (21)

Travelling

Find out if there is transport: *Kann ich mit [dem Bus] nach . . . fahren*? (15) Ask about departure times: *Wann fährt [der nächste Zug] nach . . .*? Ask about arrival times: *Wann kommt [der Bus] in . . . an*? Make a reservation: *Ich fahre [am Montag] nach . . . Ich möchte [zwei Plätze] reservieren*. (15, 21) Buy single/ return tickets, first/ second class: *[Zweimal] einfach/ hin und zurück nach . . ., erste/ zweite Klasse*. Ask where the departure point is: *Wo ist [die Bushaltestelle]*? Check you've found the right vehicle: *Ist das [die U-Bahn] nach . . .*? Ask about reduced prices: *Gibt es [Schülerfahrkarten]*?

Driving

Ask for 2-star or 4-star petrol by quantity or value: *[30] Liter Normal*. (21) *Super für [40] DM*. Get parts of your car checked: *Prüfen Sie bitte* [*den Ölstand*]! (8, 11) Say what is wrong with your vehicle: [*Die Batterie*] *ist kaputt*. Ask where you can get help: *Wo ist die nächste* [*Tankstelle*]? Ask for help in a breakdown: *Könnten Sie* [*mir bitte helfen*]? (5, 22) Say where you are: [*Mein Auto*] *steht* [*auf der Bundesstraße 5*]. (1, 15)

Shopping

Ask what shopping places are nearby: *Gibt es hier in der Nähe* [*einen Markt*]? (11) Ask where in the shop goods are: *Wo haben Sie* [*Schallplatten*] ? (21) Ask where shops/ parts of shops are: *Wo ist* [*die Sportabteilung*] ? Say what goods you'd like or ask if they have any: *Ich möchte gern/ Haben Sie* [*Kartoffeln*]. (21) Ask about prices: *Was kostet* [*die Butter*]? *Was kosten* [*die Eier*]? (1, 21) Say what quantity you want: *Ich nehme* [*sechs Scheiben Schinken*] . (1, 21, 23) Say why you don't want to buy: *Das ist zu* [*teuer*]. Ask for an alternative: *Haben Sie etwas* [*Billigeres*]? (18)

Going out

Suggest going somewhere: *Gehen wir* [*in die Diskothek*]! (7, 13) Invite somebody somewhere: *Ich gehe* [*ins Konzert*] . *Willst du mitkommen*? (5, 13) Find out what your friend wants to do: *Willst du* [*einen Film ansehen*]? (5, 11) Suggest a time and place to meet: *Treffen wir uns* [*um halb drei*] [*vor dem Freibad*]. (7, 15) Say when you'll meet again: *Auf Wiedersehen! Bis* [*später*]! (19) Find out when an event begins: *Wann beginnt* [*der Film*]? (1) Find out when an event ends: *Wann ist* [*die Party*] *zu Ende*?

Post office, phone, bank

Find out where you can phone/ post letters/ change money: *Wo ist* [*die nächste Telefonzelle*]? State your need:

Ich möchte $\begin{bmatrix} \textit{einen Brief nach . . . schicken} \\ \textit{nach . . . telefonieren} \\ \textit{einen Reisescheck einlösen} \end{bmatrix}$. (5)
.
. (11)

Find out the cost: *Was kostet* [*ein Anruf*] *nach . . .*? Buy stamps: [*Zwei*] *Briefmarken zu* [*eine Mark fünfzig*].

Accommodation

Find out if accommodation is available: *Haben Sie* [*Betten*] *für* [*zwei Mädchen*] [*bis Montag*]? (21) Say that you have reserved: *Ich habe* [*einen Platz*] *reserviert*. (9, 11) Ask where things/ people are in the camp/ hotel/ hostel: *Wo ist* [*der Herbergsvater*]? Ask where, or whether, you can do something: (*Wo*) *kann man hier* [*schlafen*]? (5) Ask about mealtimes: *Wann gibt es* [*Frühstück*] ? Say what you'd like to hire: *Ich möchte [einen Schlafsack] entleihen.* (5, 11) Ask the price: *Was kostet es pro [Tag]?* Find out what the price includes: *Ist [Bedienung] einbegriffen?*

Illness

Say how you feel: *Ich bin [krank].* (3) *Mir ist [heiß].* (22) Say how long you've been hurting where: *Ich habe seit [einer Woche] [Zahn]schmerzen.* (15) Say what you'd like to do about it: *Ich möchte [zum Zahnarzt].* (15) Ask a chemist for something for your complaint: *Haben Sie etwas gegen [Sonnenbrand]?* Say what you need: *Ich brauche [Aspirin].*

Lost property

Say what you've lost/ left behind where: *Ich habe [meinen Paß] [im Zug] vergessen.* (11, 14) Describe the lost object: *Die Tasche ist [groß] und [braun] und [aus Leder].*

Languages

Say which languages you speak/ understand: *Ich spreche/ verstehe [Deutsch].* Ask somebody to repeat, write, spell, speak more slowly, etc.: *Könnten Sie das [wiederholen]?* (5) Ask for translations: *Wie sagt man ... auf [Deutsch]?* (1) *Was bedeutet ... auf [Englisch]?*

GERMAN SPEAKING: CONVERSATION

This section contains key sentences for use in German conversation. Make use of those which apply to you, by replacing the words in brackets with words of your own (see page 24). The numbers which follow some of the German sentences refer to units in the 'Grammar' section.

People

Name: *Ich heiße ...* (1) Family: *Ich habe [einen Bruder].* (11) *[Meine ältere Schwester] heißt ...* (19) Pets: *Ich habe [einen Hund], der ... heißt.* (11, 24) Age: *Ich bin ... Jahre alt.* (3) Descriptions: *[Mein Bruder ist] ziemlich [intelligent]. Er ist [intelligenter] als [ich].* (19) *Ich habe [kurzes] [braunes] Haar.*

Leisure

Sport: *Ich bin (nicht) sportlich. Ich treibe [jeden Tag] Sport.* (1, 18) *Ich spiele gern [Tischtennis] [bei meinem Freund].* (1, 15) *Ich [schwimme] gern. Ich mag [Judo] gern.* TV, radio, etc.: *Ich sehe/ höre [drei Stunden pro Tag] Fern/ Radio.* (1) *Ich mag [Sport und Musiksendungen].* (21) Music: *Ich mag [Popmusik]. Ich spiele [Klarinette] [im Schulorchester].* (14) Hobbies: *Ich [lese] gern und ich interessiere*

49

mich für [Elektronik]. (6) Going out: *Am Samstagabend gehe ich zum Jugendklub*. (15, 16, 24)

Home

Birth: *Ich bin 19 . . . in . . . geboren. Ich bin [Engländerin]*. (10, 20) Address: *Ich wohne in . . . Das ist [eine Großstadt] im [Norden] von [England]*. (14) *Meine Adresse ist . . . Das ist [in der Stadtmitte]*. (14) Local town: *. . . ist eine [wichtige] Stadt*. (18) *Es gibt Sehenswürdigkeiten, zum Beispiel [den Hafen]*. (21) *Für sportliche Leute gibt es [ein Sportzentrum]. Zur Unterhaltung kann man [in den Park gehen]*. (13) House/ flat: *Ich wohne in [einem kleinen modernen Reihenhaus]*. (18) *Wir haben [ein Wohnzimmer] und [zwei] Schlafzimmer*. (21) *Mein Schlafzimmer ist [groß und bequem]. In meinem Schlafzimmer habe ich [meinen Radiorecorder]*. (11) Housework: *[Jeden Morgen] [mache ich mein Bett]*. (18, 24) Routine: *[Um 7 Uhr] [wache ich auf]*. (24) Recent events: *Gestern abend [bin ich zu Freunden gegangen]*. (10)

Weather, date, seasons

Day, date: *Heute ist [Montag], der [zweite Januar]*. Birthday: *Ich habe am [ersten März] Geburtstag*. (18) Weather: *Es [regnet]*. (1) Past weather: *Letzte Woche war es [sonnig]*. (24) Months, seasons: *Im [August] haben wir Ferien*. (16, 24)

Holidays

In general: *Ich fahre gern [ans Meer]*. (2, 15) Activities: *[Am Strand] [schwimme] ich gern*. (15, 24) Future: *In den nächsten Sommerferien fahre ich nach . . .* (14, 24) *Das ist [ein Dorf] [an der Küste]*. (15) *Ich fahre mit [meiner Familie]*. (15) Past holidays, trips abroad: *Ich bin [letztes Jahr] ins Ausland gefahren*. (13, 18) *Ich bin [einmal] nach Deutschland gefahren*. (10) *Ich war [zwei Wochen] [in einem Wohnwagen] [in Bayern]*. (25) *Wir sind mit [dem Auto] gefahren*. (10, 15) *Wir haben [München] besichtigt*. (9) *[Die Landschaft] hat mir gefallen*. (9, 22)

Work

School: *Meine Schule heißt . . . Schule*. (1) *Sie liegt [nicht weit von meinem Haus]*. (15) *Ich komme [zu Fuß] zur Schule*. (16, 25) *Ich esse zu Mittag [zu Hause]. Wir haben [ein Schwimmbad und einen Sportplatz]*. (12) *Wir haben [500 Schülerinnen]*. (20) School work: *Ich lerne [Englisch, Chemie . . .]. Mein bestes Fach ist [Sport]*. (18) *Ich bin in der [zehnten] Klasse*. (14) *In der [Oberstufe] möchte ich [Soziologie] lernen*. (14, 24) Future plans: *Ich werde [zur Hochschule gehen]*. (15) *Ich möchte [Köchin] werden*. (17, 20) *Ich möchte [in einem Restaurant] arbeiten*. (14) Jobs in family: *[Mein Vater] ist [Arzt]*. (17) *[Meine*

Mutter] *arbeitet* [*bei einer Firma*]. (15) Part-time jobs: *Ich arbeite* [*samstags*] [*bei einem Supermarkt*]. (15) *Ich bekomme . . . Pfund pro Stunde. Ich kaufe* [*Kleider und Schallplatten*]. (21) Dreams: *Ich spare mein Geld, um* [*ein Moped*] *zu kaufen.* (1) *Wenn ich reich wäre, würde ich* [*ein großes Haus kaufen*]. (5, 18)

Opinions

Likes and preferences:

$$
Ich \begin{bmatrix} wohne \\ esse \\ spiele \\ lese \end{bmatrix} \begin{bmatrix} gern \\ lieber \\ am\ liebsten \\ night\ gern \end{bmatrix} \quad \begin{array}{l} [auf\ dem\ Lande]\ .\ (1, 15) \\ [Pommes\ frites]\ .\ (19) \\ [Tennis]\ . \\ [Science\ Fiction]\ . \end{array}
$$

Favourites: *Meine Lieblings* [*sendung*] *heißt* . . . (12) Reasons: *Mein Lieblings* [*sport*] *ist* [*Angeln*], *weil es* [*ruhig*] *ist.* (24)

GERMAN GRAMMAR

This section deals with basic grammar rules which crop up in sentences in the 'Speaking' sections (see page 24).

Examples

1
Ich treibe jeden Tag Sport.
Ich spiele gern Tischtennis.
Ich lerne Englisch und Chemie.
In den nächsten Sommerferien fahre ich nach Bognor.
Ich nehme eine Tasse Kaffee.
Was kosten die Eier?
Es regnet.
Meine Mutter arbeitet bei einer Firma.

2
Ich fahre gern ans Meer.
Wann fährt der nächste Zug nach Bonn?

3
Ich bin sechzehn Jahre alt.
Mein Bruder ist intelligent.

Grammar notes

These sentences are about something happening *regularly*, or *now*, or
soon, so they are in the PRESENT TENSE. The present tense ends in **e** with **ich**,
en if the subject is plural (e.g. the egg**s**),
and **t** with *he, she* or *it*.

Verbs which change their vowel sound (here **a** → **ä**) are called STRONG VERBS.

IRREGULAR VERBS don't follow a pattern. These examples are from **sein** (to be).

4

Ich habe *kurzes braunes Haar.*
Wir haben *zwei Schlafzimmer.*
Haben *Sie etwas Billigeres?*

These sentences contain parts of **haben** (to have).

5

Ich möchte *in einem Restaurant arbeit*en.
Darf *ich meine Eltern anruf*en*?*
Willst *du mitkomm*en*?*
Kann *ich das Rathaus besichtigen?*
Könnten Sie *mir bitte helf*en*?*
Könnten Sie *das wiederhol*en*?*
Ich werde *zur Hochschule geh*en.

Wenn ich reich wäre, würde *ich ein großes Haus kauf*en.

These **en** endings, which sometimes translate as 'to', are IN-FINITIVES, which go at the *end* of the phrase or sentence. They are used after: **möchte** (would like) from the verb **mögen;**
darf (allowed to) from **dürfen;**
will, etc. (want) from **wollen;**
kann (can) from **können;**

könnten Sie (could you, would you) also from **können;**
werde (shall) from **werden,** to form the FUTURE TENSE;
würde (should) also from **werden,** to form the CONDITION-AL TENSE.

6
Ich interessiere mich *für Elektronik.*

This sentence contains **mich** because the verb is REFLEX-IVE.

7
*Geh*en wir *in die Diskothek!*
*Treff*en wir *uns um halb drei!*

–en wir . . .! is an IMPERATIVE meaning, 'Let's . . .!'

8
*Prüf*en Sie *bitte das Wasser!*

–en Sie . . .! is an IMPERATIVE giving a command. Other examples: *Geh*en Sie *hier geradeaus. Nehm*en Sie *die erste Straße links.*

9
Wir haben *München besichtigt.*
Ich habe *ein Zimmer reserviert.*
Wir haben *den Schwarzwald gesehen.*
Die Landschaft hat *mir gefallen.*
Ich habe *meinen Paß vergessen.*

These sentences about the past are in the PERFECT TENSE, formed from part of **haben** with a past participle which ends in **t** or **en**, usually begins with **ge** and goes at the *end* of the sentence.

10

Ich **bin** *1972 in London* **gebor**en.
Gestern abend **bin** *ich zu Freun-*
den **gegang**en.
Wir **sind** *mit dem Auto* **gefahr**en.

A few verbs form the PERFECT
TENSE by using part of **sein**
instead of **haben**.

11

Prüfen Sie bitte **den** *Ölstand!*
Ich habe **einen** *Bruder.*
Ich habe **mein**en *Paß vergessen.*
Ich möchte **einen** *Brief nach*
England schicken.
Willst du **einen** *Film ansehen?*
Gibt es hier in der Nähe **einen**
Markt?

ARTICLES (the, a) and POS-
SESSIVES (my, etc.) end in **en**
before MASCULINE nouns (*der*
*Ölstand, der Bruder, der Pa*ß) in
the ACCUSATIVE.

Es gibt (there is) is always followed by an accusative.

12

Wann ist **die** *Sparkasse geöffnet?*
Ich nehme **eine** *Tasse Kaffee.*
Kann ich **das** *Rathaus besichti-*
gen?
Gibt es hier in der Nähe **ein**
Freibad?

'The', 'a' and 'my' are **die,**
eine, meine before FEMININE
nouns (*Sparkasse, Tasse*) and
das, ein, mein before NEUTER
nouns (*Rathaus, Freibad*), whether accusative or nominative.

13

Zur Unterhaltung kann man **in**
den *Park gehen.*
Gehen wir **in die** *Diskothek!*
Ich bin letztes Jahr **ins** *Ausland*
gefahren.

The ACCUSATIVE is used after
the PREPOSITION **in** when
there is *movement into* something.
ins = in das

14

In *meinem Schlafzimmer habe*
ich meinen Radiorecorder.
Ich möchte **in** *einem Restaurant*
arbeiten.

Was gibt es **in** *der Stadt zu tun?*
Mein Haus ist **in** *der Stadtmitte.*
Leeds ist **im** *Norden von Eng-*
land.

But when there is no movement,
in is followed by the DATIVE,
and the words for 'the', 'a', 'my'
are:
dem, einem, meinem (masculine,
neuter);
der, einer, meiner (feminine).
im = in dem

15

Ich möchte zum *Zahnarzt.*
Ich komme zu Fuß zur *Schule.*
Kann ich mit dem *Bus fahren?*
Ich fahre mit meiner *Familie.*
Am Strand schwimme ich gern.
Das ist ein Dorf an der *Küste.*

Other PREPOSITIONS. The DATIVE is also used after **zu** (**zum** = **zu dem**, **zur** = **zu der**); after **mit**:

after **an**, unless there is movement, e.g. *Ich fahre gern* **ans** *Meer.* (**ans** = **an das**, **am** = **an dem**);

Ich spiele gern Tischtennis bei meinem *Freund.*
Meine Mutter arbeitet bei einer *Firma.*

after **bei** (meaning 'at' or 'in' a place of work or someone's home);

Ich wohne gern auf dem *Lande.*
Mein Auto steht auf der *Bundesstraße 5.*

after **auf** (usually);

Die Schule ist nicht weit von meinem *Haus.*

and after **von**,

Treffen wir uns vor dem *Freibad.*
Ich habe seit einer *Woche Zahnschmerzen.*

vor (usually),
and **seit**.

16

Ich komme zu Fuß zur *Schule.*
Kann ich mit dem *Bus fahren?*
Im August haben wir Ferien.
Ich fahre am *Montag nach Bonn.*

DEFINITE ARTICLES (words for 'the') are often used in German where they would be omitted in English.

17

Ich möchte Köchin werden.
Mein Vater ist Arzt.

INDEFINITE ARTICLES (words for 'a') are omitted in German when talking about jobs and professions.

18

letzte Woche
letztes Jahr
jeden Tag
Guten Appetit!
Gute Reise!

When ADJECTIVES go before the noun they describe, they usually end in **e, en** or **es**. Expressions of time, and 'Good . . .', are ACCUSATIVE, with the same endings as the words for 'the'.

Ich wohne in einem kleinen modernen Reihenhaus.
In den nächsten Sommerferien, fahre ich nach Bognor.
Ich habe am ersten März Geburtstag.
Wann fährt der nächste Zug?
Leeds ist eine wichtige Stadt.
Für sportliche Leute gibt es ein Sportzentrum.
Mein bestes Fach ist Sport.
Ich habe kurzes braunes Haar.

These adjectives are in the DATIVE because they follow **in** and **an**. The dative adjective ending is **en**.

Otherwise, adjectives describing something or someone masculine, feminine, or
plural often end in **e**;
and adjectives describing something neuter often end in **es**.

19
Ich esse lieber Pommes frites.
Bis später!
Meine ältere Schwester heißt . . .

Mein Bruder ist intelligenter als ich.

COMPARATIVE ADJECTIVES
are formed by adding **er**,
and sometimes an umlaut as well,
plus the usual endings before a noun.
In comparisons, 'than' is **als**.

20
Hier ist meine Freundin Paula.
Ich möchte Köchin werden.
Wir haben 500 Schülerinnen.

Words for males can be made FEMININE by adding **in** and sometimes an umlaut too. The plural ending is **innen**.

21

Liter, Zimmer, Eis, Kuchen
Kartoffeln, Betten, Sendungen, Wochen, Stunden, Karten, Scheiben, Schallplatten, Briefmarken
Eier, Kleider
Ich esse gern Pommes frites.
Ich spiele gern Videospiele.
Ich habe zwei Brüder.
Ich möchte zwei Plätze reservieren.

Some German NOUNS are the same in the singular and the PLURAL;
a lot add **en** or **n**,
especially if the singular ends in **e**;

a few add **er**;
a few add **s**;
some add **e**;
some add an umlaut;
some add **e** and an umlaut.
Be prepared: look up any plurals you are likely to need (sisters? guinea-pigs? cassettes?)

Treffen wir uns bei **mir**.
Könnten Sie **mir** *bitte helfen?*
Die Landschaft hat **mir** *gefallen*.
Mir *ist heiß*.

Mir is the PRONOUN 'me' after prepositions which take a dative; with **helfen** (to help) and **gefallen** (to please); and in the phrases **Mir ist heiß/ kalt/ übel**, for English 'I am . . .'

23
Noch eine Tasse Kaffee!
Ich nehme sechs Scheiben Schinken.

In expressions of QUANTITY, German omits a word for 'of'.

24
Wann **fährt** *der nächste Zug nach Bonn?*
Was **kostet** *die Butter?*

Am Strand **schwimme** *ich gern.*
Um sieben Uhr **wache** *ich auf.*
Wenn *ich reich* **wäre** . . .
Mein Lieblingssport ist Angeln, **weil** *es ruhig* **ist**.
Ich habe einen Hund, **der** *Prinz* **heißt**.

WORD ORDER. The VERB is often the *second* idea in a sentence. This happens in sentences beginning with question words like **wann, was;** or a phrase telling 'where' or 'when'.
The verb goes to the *end* after **wenn** (if); **weil** (because); and **der, die,** or **das** when they mean 'who' or 'which'.

25
Treffen wir uns **um halb drei**| **vor dem Freibad.**
Gestern abend *bin ich* **zu Freunden** *gegangen.*
Ich war **zwei Wochen**| **in einem Wohnwagen in Bayern.**
Ich komme **zu Fuß**| **zur Schule.**
Kann ich **mit dem Bus**| **nach Bonn** *fahren?*

WORD ORDER. Phrases of TIME (when?), MANNER (how?) and PLACE (where?) go in that order: time, manner, place. These are examples of time before place.
These are examples of manner before place.

GERMAN: LISTENING AND READING

This section doesn't attempt to tell you everything you need to know to understand German. It gives some short cuts and ideas for you to think about and bear in mind and try to add to for yourself. The answers to the quizzes are on page 64.

Sound patterns

The meanings of many German words are easily guessed because they *look* similar to the English: *bringen, finden, warm, beginnen* and *Arm* are obvious. Some words *sound* similar to the English: *hier, Preis, Maus, Haus, Fisch, mein, Reis, Schuh, Banane.* But some words which *look* similar may *sound* rather unfamiliar because of differences in the sound patterns between the two languages. Think about (or find out) the German pronunciation of these letters:

ater as in *Vater*	**oo** as in *Boot*
eter as in *Peter*	**sch** as in *Schule*
g as in *Georg*	**th** as in *Apotheke*
j as in *ja*	**w** as in *Wein*
ng as in *Menge*	**z** as in *Zigarre*
sp at the beginning, as in *spielen*	
ion at the end, as in *Station*	
d, g, b at the end, as in *Abend, Tag, halb*	

Quiz 1

Underline the letters which will sound different in German from English:

Finger	*Hand*	*Religion*	*Theater*
Geographie	*Januar*	*Sport*	*warm*
Gold	*Portion*	*Schottland*	*Zoo*

Quiz 2

Other words which look similar may be hard to catch when you hear them because the stress falls on a different syllable; English **fam**ily, German *Fa**mi**lie* is an example. See if you can underline the stressed syllable in each of these words:

Appetit	*August*	*Kilometer*	*Präsident*
April	*Biologie*	*Orchester*	*Pullover*
Artikel	*Insekt*	*Person*	

Patterns linking German and English

Here are some similarities between English and German. They occur often enough to help you guess or remember the meanings of many words.

Quiz 3

Read through the examples, then find some others from the lists underneath and write them down. (There won't be equal numbers of words on each line.)

German	English	Examples
b	f, v	*Kalb, halb, lieben, — — — — — —*
ch	gh	*hoch, lachen, Licht, — — — — — —*
ch	k	*machen, Kuchen, Buch,— — — — — —*
d or *t*	th	*Mutter, denken, Leder, — — — — — —*
ei	o	*heiß, ein, meistens, — — — — — —*
f	p	*öffnen, hoffen, Schaf, — — — — — —*
g	y	*Augen, gestern, sonnig, — — — — — —*
pf	p	*Apfel, Pflaume, Pfirsich, — — — — — —*
sch	sh	*Fisch, Schuh, frisch, — — — — — —*
ss, ß	t	*heiß, beißen, besser, — — — — — —*
t	d	*Tür, unter, laut, — — — — — —*
v	f	*vier, Volk, voll, Vorname, — — — — — —*
w	w	*Wagen, was, West, — — — — — —*
z	t	*zehn, zu, Herz, — — — — — —*

Each of the following words fits *one* of the patterns above. You'll need to look up the meanings, if you don't know them already, before you can assign them to a line.

Affe	*dies*	*Laub*	*Nachbar*	*schlafen*
allein	*Honig*	*Milch*	*Salz*	*selber*

Each of these words fits *two* of the patterns above. Write them on both the relevant lines if there is room:

beide	*Pflanze*	*Tod*	*Waffe*
Dieb	*Schiff*	*Tropfen*	*waschen*
durstig	*Seife*	*Vater*	*Wasser*
heilig	*taub*	*verboten*	*Weg*
Pfad	*tief*	*vorwärts*	*weiß*
Pfeife	*Tochter*	*wachen*	

Quiz 4

Sometimes these sound patterns don't quite work, because the meanings of the related words have diverged over centuries. But with a little imagination you can see a connection, which might help you remember the modern meaning.

Fill in the meanings of the German words below. Look them up if you don't know them. The first is done for you.

German word	Related English word	Meaning of German word
Bein	bone	leg
Tier	deer	— — — — —
weit	wide	— — — — —
Gürtel	girdle	— — — — —
Herbst	harvest	— — — — —
Fleisch	flesh	— — — — —
Hafen	haven	— — — — —
kleben	cleave	— — — — —
Schwein	swine	— — — — —
tragen	draw, drag	— — — — —
Vogel	fowl	— — — — —

False friends

Some words don't have the meaning which their appearance suggests.

Quiz 5

Match each of these to one of the meanings in the brackets overleaf. Look words up if you don't know them.

Apparat	— — — — —	*Note*	— — — — —
bald	— — — — —	*paar*	— — — — —
bekommen	— — — — —	*See*	— — — — —
fast	— — — — —	*Stock*	— — — — —
Gift	— — — — —	*wenn*	— — — — —
Gymnasium	— — — — —	*wer*	— — — — —
Mappe	— — — — —	*will*	— — — — —
Maschine	— — — — —	*wo*	— — — — —
meinen	— — — — —		

almost	if	plane	think
briefcase	lake	poison	want
few	mark	secondary school	where
floor	phone	soon	who
get			

Prefixes

Many puzzling German words are simply short familiar words hiding behind a prefix or suffix or both.

Quiz 6

Match these words beginning with **Ge, er, be, ver** to one of the meanings underneath. You should be able to do it without a dictionary if you use your knowledge plus your brains.

Gebirge	– – – – –	*beantworten*	– – – – –
Gefühl	– – – – –	*verbessern*	– – – – –
Getränke	– – – – –	*verbilligen*	– – – – –
erreichen	– – – – –	*verdünnen*	– – – – –
erneuern	– – – – –	*vereinigen*	– – – – –
erkranken	– – – – –	*Verspätung*	– – – – –
erkennen	– – – – –	*verkleiden*	– – – – –

answer	disguise	feeling	mountains	recognise
cheapen	drinks	improve	reach	unite
dilute	fall ill	lateness	renew	

Quiz 7

Some prefixes have a meaning. Read the examples, then complete each line with one of the words from the bracketed list on the next page.

Prefix	Idea	Examples	Example + meaning
ab	away	*abfliegen, Absender*	*abfahren:* – – – – –
auf	up	*aufgeben, aufwachen*	*Aufzug:* – – – – –
aus	out	*Aussicht, ausverkauft*	*Ausgang:* – – – – –
ein	in	*einbrechen, Eingang*	*Einwohner:* – – – – –
ein	one	*einfach, einmal*	*Einzelzimmer:* – – – – –
un	un	*unfreundlich, unmöglich*	*Unglück:* – – – – –
vor	before	*Vormittag, vorbereiten*	*Vorwählnummer:* – – – – –
weg	(a)way	*wegwerfen, weggehen*	*Wegweiser:* – – – – –

depart	exit	lift	single room
dialling code	inhabitant	misfortune	signpost

Suffixes

Suffix	Use, meaning	Examples
chen	little	*Bröt*chen (roll); *Kätz*chen (kitten)
tens	-ly	*ers*tens (firstly); *meis*tens (mostly)
mal	how many times	*ein*mal (once); *manch*mal (sometimes)
ung *keit*	indicate nouns	*Send*ung (programme) *Schwierig*keiten (difficulties)
isch *lich*	indicate adjectives	*prakt*isch (practical) *täg*lich (daily)
los	-less, un	*atem*los (breathless); *arbeits*los (unemployed)
er	belonging to a town	*Hamburg*er (from Hamburg)
s	what (part of) day	*montag*s (on Mondays); *abend*s (in the evenings)
iert	-ed	*reserv*iert (reserved)

Compounds

German words combine not only with prefixes and suffixes but also with other words. Once you know a few short, important syllables, you have access to the meanings of countless compound words. For instance:

German syllable	Idea	Examples
stell	place	**Stell**e (job); **stell**en (to place); *Bau***stell**e (building site); *Tank***stell**e (petrol station)
schaf	do	**Schaff**ner (manager); *be***schäf**tigt *(busy)*; *G***eschäf**t (business)
fall	event	*Un***fall** (accident); *Zwischen***fall** (incident); **fall**s (in case)
teil	part	*Ab***teil** (compartment); *Ab***teil**ung (department); **teil***nehmen* (to take part); *Stadt***teil** (part of town)

Quiz 8

Can you fit the following words to the translations underneath, without using a dictionary? You'll need to know the meaning of most of the 'bricks' which build up the German words, and think what the English really means.

Arbeitgeber	– – – – –	*schamrot*	– – – – –
bewaffnet	– – – – –	*Speisewagen*	– – – – –
erklären	– – – – –	*Staatsangehörigkeit*	– – – – –
Fußgängerzone	– – – – –	*Tiefkühltruhe*	– – – – –
Gepäckträger	– – – – –	*vorgestern*	– – – – –
Neuigkeit	– – – – –	*Wettervorhersage*	– – – – –
preiswert	– – – – –	*wirklichkeitstreu*	– – – – –

armed	explain	porter
blushing	nationality	realistic
deep freeze	novelty	two days ago
dining-car	of good value	weather forecast
employer	pedestrian precinct	

Understand words in the sentence

Make use of grammatical markers, especially in 'Higher Reading'. For instance, remember that word order in German can be very different from English, so beware of accusatives and datives which may begin the sentence but are not the subject of the verb.

Quiz 9

Underline who or what . . .

1 saw: *Den Jungen hat der Fisch gesehen.*

2 gave: *Seinem Onkel gab Peter gar nichts.*

3 showed: *Das neue Haus zeigten sie den Freunden.*

Also notice clues which indicate plurals or feminines. Who is in the classroom in this sentence?

Die Schülerin spielt in der Klasse.

A boy? A girl? Boys? Girls? *Die* can indicate either feminine or plural, so it's not one boy. The *in* ending of *Schülerin* indicates a female, so it's not boys. *Spielt* has a singular ending, so it can't be girls.

Watch out for past participles, usually beginning with *ge* or ending with *iert*, often '-ed' in English, and present participles, ending with *end*, '-ing' in English. They may have extra endings if they are being used as adjectives. Here are some examples from specimen exam papers:

zwei mit Pistolen bewaffnete Männer
(two men arm*ed* with pistols)

Achtung! Der aus Köln kommende Zug . . .
(the train arri*ving* from Cologne . . .)
(Southern Examining Group, Extended Reading and Listening)

Now look at this

Here is a text from a specimen exam paper. You don't need to understand *all* the words, but just see how many you know. Everything in bold print is either:

> obvious from its similarity to English;
> or a name;
> or has been dealt with in this section.

The text comes under a photo of a young woman in jeans and shirt playing with two ape cubs:

> *Leute von heute, von sich* selbst **fotografiert. Diesmal: Jutta Seidel, 21, Tier***pfleger***in in *der* **Stuttgarter Wilhelma, Abteilung** *Menschen-* **affen.** *Dort sorgt sie u.a. für die* gute *Kinderstube* **dieser beiden Gorilla-***Knilche* name*ns* **Obsus und Ulca.** *Ihren* **Affen** *gibt sie nicht etwa Zucker, sondern um 6 Uhr* **Milch** *oder Ovo; später Obst, Gemüse,* **Laub**; *mittags* **bekommen** *sie einen Griesbrei mit* **Honig,** *nach***mittags** *noch***mal Milch und abends eine Banane. Jutta Seidel** *macht, was sie* **will.** *Und sie* **trägt,** *was ihr pa*ß*t:* **Jeans und Shirts.**
> (Northern Examining Association, Basic Reading)

The text also has an example of a sentence beginning with a dative: **Ihren Affen gibt sie** . . . It's Jutta who is giving, of course, not the apes.

Feel the sense

A major aid to understanding is to develop a *feel* for meaning. A disturbed third-year boy called Martin once asked to take German as an exam option, but his work was so minimal that it was hard to tell whether he had any aptitude for German or not. The teacher soon found out − on the day the class met the word *Schlager* (hit record). Martin was at once reminded of a phrase he had met previously meaning 'the clock strikes'. 'It's like *die Turmuhr schlägt,*' he said. The others in the group were baffled: they pointed out that clocks don't hit, and records aren't strikes, and anyway ä is not the same as **a**, so the words had nothing in common. Only Martin could see that 'hit' and 'strike' are connected in meaning even if they aren't interchangeable in English, and that the change in the vowel didn't affect the link in meaning. Martin went on to cope quite well with the 'O' level 'Reading' paper, but he would have done better in GCSE, where his kind of instinctive feel for meaning would have been valued more highly.

So, keep your mind open for links, *even* if there are vowel changes, as in *trinken/Getränke* (common idea: 'drink') or *Eintritt/betreten* ('tread'); *even* if the connecting idea becomes tenuous, as in *Schluß* (end), *schließlich* (finally), *geschlossen* (closed); *even* if you have to invent an English equivalent: *beißen* is 'to bite', so your brain should register *ein bissiger Hund* as 'a bitey dog', although 'bitey' doesn't exist and can't be used.

Use your knowledge of English. For instance, you know the meaning of the English word 'bind', so the meaning of *Verbindung* (connection, communication) should be easy to remember. What does 'to wax' mean, as in 'wax and wane'? If you know, you'll have no trouble with *wachsen* and *Erwachsene*. *Mitte* and *mittel* mean 'middle', the middle may also be the mean, so *Lebensmittel* is the 'means of staying alive', simply 'food'.

ANSWERS

Quiz 1

*F*inger, *G*eogra*phie*, *G*ol*d*, *H*an*d*, *J*anuar, *P*or*ti*on, *R*eli*gi*on, *S*port, *Sch*ottlan*d*, *Th*e*a*ter, *w*arm, *Z*oo

Quiz 2

*A*ppe*t*it, *A*pril, *A*r*t*ikel, *A*u*g*ust, *Bio*lo*gi*e, *In*sekt, *Ki*lo*me*ter, *Or*ches*t*er, *P*er*s*on, *P*räsi*d*ent, *Pu*llover

Quiz 3

b	f, v	*Laub* (leaves, foliage), *selber, Dieb, taub*
ch	gh	*Nachbar, Tochter*
ch	k	*Milch, wachen*
d or *t*	th	*dies, beide, Dieb, durstig, Pfad, Tod, Vater*
ei	o	*allein, beide, heilig, Seife*
f	p	*Affe, schlafen, Pfeife, Schiff, Seife, tief, Waffe*
g	y	*Honig, durstig, heilig, Weg*
pf	p	*Pfad, Pfeife, Pflanze, Tropfen*
sch	sh	*Schiff, waschen*
ss, ß	t	*Wasser, weiß*
t	d	*taub, tief, Tochter, Tod, Tropfen, verboten*
v	f	*Vater, verboten, vorwärts*
w	w	*vorwärts, wachen, Waffe, waschen, Wasser, Weg, weiß*
z	t	*Salz, Pflanze*

Quiz 4

Tier: animal; *weit:* far; *Gürtel:* belt; *Herbst:* autumn; *Fleisch:* meat; *Hafen:* port; *kleben:* to stick; *Schwein:* pig; *tragen:* wear, carry; *Vogel:* bird.

Quiz 5

Apparat: phone (*am Apparat:* speaking); *bald:* soon; *bekommen:* get; *fast:* almost; *Gift:* poison; *Gymnasium:* secondary school; *Mappe:* briefcase; *Maschine:* plane; *meinen:* think (as in *Was meinst du?* What do you think?); *Note:* mark; *paar:* few; *See:* lake; *Stock:* floor, storey of building; *wenn:* if; *wer:* who; *will:* want; *wo:* where.

Quiz 6

Gebirge: mountains; *Gefühl:* feeling; *Getränke:* drinks; *erreichen:* reach; *erneuern:* renew; *erkranken:* fall ill; *erkennen:* recognise; *beantworten:* to answer; *verbessern:* improve; *verbilligen:* cheapen; *verdünnen:* dilute ('thin' a liquid); *vereinigen:* unite (*Vereinigten Staaten:* USA); *Verspätung:* lateness; *verkleiden:* disguise.

Quiz 7

abfahren: to depart; *Aufzug:* lift; *Ausgang:* exit; *Einwohner:* inhabitant; *Einzelzimmer:* single room; *Unglück:* misfortune; *Vorwählnummer:* dialling code ('before-choose-number'); *Wegweiser:* signpost.

Quiz 8

Arbeitgeber: employer ('work-giver'); *bewaffnet:* armed ('be-weapon-ed'); *erklären:* explain ('make clear'); *Fußgängerzone:* pedestrian precinct ('foot-goer-zone'); *Gepäckträger:* porter ('pack-carrier'); *Neuigkeit:* novelty ('newness'); *preiswert:* of good value ('price-worthy'); *schamrot:* blushing ('shame-red'); *Speisewagen:* dining-car; *Staatsangehörigkeit:* nationality ('state's-belongingness'); *Tiefkühltruhe:* deep freeze ('deep cool chest'); *vorgestern:* two days ago ('before yesterday'); *Wettervorhersage:* weather forecast ('weather-beforehand-saying'); *wirklichkeitstreu:* realistic ('reality-true').

Quiz 9

1 The fish saw: *den Jungen* is accusative. **2** Peter gave: *seinem Onkel* is dative, '*to* his uncle'. **3** The verb ends in *en*, so it's plural, so either *sie* or *den Freunden* showed. But *den Freunden* is dative plural, so *sie* is the subject: 'They showed the new house to the friends.'

GERMAN: WRITING LETTERS

Learn all these phrases and test yourself by covering the German words and working from the English (see page 25).

All words for *you* and *your* must start with *capitals* in a letter:

Du, Dich, Dir, Dein in informal letters;
Sie, Ihnen, Ihr in formal letters.

Informal letters

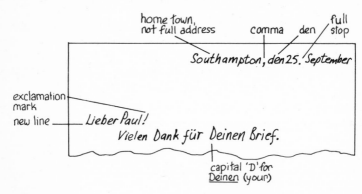

Beginning

Lieber . . . !	Dear (writing to a boy)
Liebe . . . !	Dear (writing to a girl)
Vielen Dank für Deinen Brief.	Thanks very much for your letter.

Ending

Schreib bald wieder!	Write back soon.
Alles Gute	Best wishes
Dein	Yours, (if you're a boy)
Deine	Yours, (if you're a girl)

Formal letters

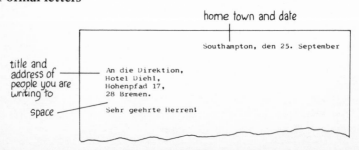

Beginning

Sehr geehrte Herren!   Dear Sir,

Middle

Ich möchte $\begin{bmatrix} Sie\ um \ldots bitten \\ gern\ wissen, \ldots \\ ein \ldots entleihen \end{bmatrix}.$ I'd like to $\begin{bmatrix} ask\ you\ for \ldots \\ know, \ldots \\ hire\ a \ldots \end{bmatrix}$

Ich bitte Sie,
mir ein... zu $\begin{bmatrix} reservieren \\ geben \end{bmatrix}.$ Please would you $\begin{bmatrix} reserve \\ give \end{bmatrix}$ me a ...

Ich wäre sehr dankbar, wenn   I'd be very grateful if

Sie mir... $\begin{bmatrix} empfehlen \\ schicken \end{bmatrix}$ *könnten.*   you could $\begin{bmatrix} recommend \\ send \end{bmatrix}$ me ...

Ending

Hochachtungsvoll,   Yours sincerely,

SECTION 3

Practising for the exam

LISTENING: HINTS AND TIPS

Here are some ideas to help you tackle the 'Listening' paper.

1 *Read* the instructions and questions in English, before you hear the recording. Notice clues about what to expect. For instance, look at this question from a 'Basic' level paper:

> **The train you are travelling on arrives in Tours and you hear an announcement. How long does the train stop in Tours?**
>
> **5 minutes   10 minutes   15 minutes   20 minutes**
>
> **(Midland Examining Group, French)**

So before you hear the tape at all, you know that it's going to mention five, or ten, or fifteen, or twenty minutes, and that's what you'll be listening for.

2 Write your answers *after* you've heard the recording. If you write *during* the recording, you'll miss bits, because writing is slower than speaking. This is obvious, but you'd be surprised how many candidates have been seen happily writing the answer to question **1** while the tape is giving the information for questions **2–5**. Then they sit looking stupid during the pause provided for answering questions **1–5**!

3 However, it's sometimes helpful, especially at 'Higher' level, to *make notes* during the recording, if you are told that you may. In the following task, 'Higher' candidates hear quite a long interview with a French lady living in England. These questions follow:

> *1* **When and why did the lady leave her native France?**
> **(3 marks)**
>
> *2* **Who was disturbed in the night, and why?**
> **(2 marks)**
>
> *3* **Which drink did everybody have for breakfast?**
> **(1 mark)**
>
> *4* **Why did the friend not eat breakfast with the family?**
> **(1 mark)**

5 Why is her friend not at work at the moment?
(1 mark)

(Southern Examining Group, French)

There's a lot to remember here, so notes might help. For instance, the answer to number **1** is: She married (1 mark) an Englishman (1 mark) who works in England (1 mark). *During* the recording you might quickly scribble on your rough paper:

① mar Eng.man, wks Eng

After the recording you'll be given time to re-write the note so that it makes sense to the examiner.
4 You *don't* have to answer in full sentences, provided that what you have written is clear and complete. The answer to question **3** is: Tea. That's all you need write for your mark. There's no need to waste good thinking-time writing: 'The drink which everybody had for breakfast was tea.'

Notice that there is an important difference between:

making notes;
answering in note form;
answering in full sentences.

Here is an example, using question **2** above. The interviewee tells us that her baby is teething, and she had to get up to her twice in the night. Father slept through, as usual.

Notes:
mum – baby cried

Answer in note form:
Mother, because her baby cried.

Answer in full sentence:
The mother was disturbed in the night because her baby cried.

Unless you are told otherwise, the answer in note form is what's expected. The words 'in note form' are a bit confusing, so think of this as meaning: 'in conversational form'. Imagine yourself in a situation where a French/German speaker has just said something and at your elbow, your non-linguistic friend is pestering you to explain: 'What did he say?' 'What was all that about?' So you ask the speaker to say it again, and then you tell your friend as much as necessary for him to follow the conversation – not every word, but the important parts. In the exam, the 'speaker' is the tape, your 'friend' is the examiner, you hear a repeat once you know what he wants you to tell him, and you answer as you would in a conversation.

5 During the pause between the first and second hearings, you can read through the questions again and/or answer what you can. Then, by the time you hear the repeat, you should know *exactly* what you need to find out, and you can concentrate on the relevant parts of the recording. In the same interview, the French woman tells us a lot about where she comes from, what the family eats for breakfast and what the friend does for a living. None of this helps with the questions. By the second hearing, you'll know that you can relax during those parts.

LISTENING PRACTICE

If you know anyone able and willing to read the language you are studying, try the specimen tasks below like this:

(a) Read the questions.
(b) Get your assistant to read the passage underneath.
(c) Repeat (a) and (b).
(d) Write your answers, and mark them from page 73.

If you're on your own, pretend as best you can.

French Basic

This task, from the middle of a 'Basic Listening' specimen paper, is probably of average difficulty for 'Basic' level. There are two speakers on the recording, a young man and a girl.

QUESTIONS

(a) **What day does the young man suggest for the outing?**

(b) **What choice of outing does the young man suggest?**
   Answer: **They could either . . . or . . . .**

(c) **What condition does the girl make for going on the outing?**
   Answer: **She will go if . . .**

(d) **Tick ONE of these statements that you think best describes the girl's attitude:**
   She is keen to go out with the boy.
   She is not particularly bothered about going out
   with the boy.
   She is too busy to think of going out.
   She is upset that the boy has asked her out.

(Northern Examining Association)

TRANSCRIPT OF RECORDING

   Boy: Tu veux sortir avec moi, samedi?
   Girl: Bof, ça dépend. Où est-ce qu'on va?

Boy: *À la plage, si tu veux? Ou à la campagne?*
Qu'est-ce que tu veux?

Girl: *Bon, à la plage, peut-être . . . C'est possible . . .*
S'il fait beau.

Boy: *Mais, écoute! On ne sait jamais, s'il va faire beau. On sort*
samedi, oui ou non?

Girl: *S'il fait beau, je te dis. Parce que moi, s'il ne fait pas beau, je*
préfère rester seule à la maison.

French Higher

This task is taken from near the end of a 'Higher' specimen paper. In the recording, the speaker is trying to remember an incident which happened many years ago. It's very natural speech. When she searches for the words to express herself, she pauses, or says, 'Euh . . .'. Like many French people, she repeats words to give herself time to choose the word which comes next.

QUESTIONS

You will hear a young French woman telling about her most vivid memory from her first trip to London. Listen to see if you can grasp the main points of the story. Answer each question with ONE short phrase or sentence in English.

(a) Where did this incident happen?

(b) How old was she at the time?

(c) What unfortunate thing happened?

(d) What did she do about it?

(Northern Examining Association)

TRANSCRIPT OF RECORDING

La première fois que je suis venue en Angleterre, c'était il y a . . . une dixaine d'années, je suis . . . allée à l'hôtel Victoria à Londres, et c'est un hôtel immense avec quelque chose comme cinq cents chambres, et j'avais . . . une douzaine d'années à l'époque, j'avais fait à peine . . . très peu d'anglais. Et dans cet hôtel, les, les portes se ferment, euh, de l'intérieur. Et on nous avait dit: «Faites attention, euh, de ne pas vous fermer dehors,» et c'est ce qui m'est arrivé. Je suis partie de la chambre et . . . la porte s'est refermée et j'étais complètement perdue, je ne savais pas où était mon professeur, je parlais très peu anglais. Alors, il a fallu que j'aille toute seule au bureau des réclamations, essayer d'expliquer . . . que . . . j'étais fermée dehors, que j'étais Française et que . . . je ne savais pas quoi faire. Bon, ça fait partie des, des souvenirs de ce premier séjour en Angleterre . . .

C'est un, c'est un beau souvenir finalement, ça, m'a obligée à, à me débrouiller en anglais.

German Basic

This extract is from the end of a specimen 'Basic' paper, and is probably the hardest task on the paper. There are two speakers on this recording, a post-office employee and a customer.

QUESTIONS

You are in a post-office in Germany. Listen to the conversation and then answer the questions.

(a) What does the customer wish to do in addition to buying stamps? (2 marks)

(b) How much will it cost to do this? (1 mark)

(c) What information must be given on the form? (2 marks)

(Northern Examining Association)

TRANSCRIPT OF RECORDING

Customer: *Geben Sie mir bitte zwei Briefmarken zu 90 Pfennig. Ich möchte auch dieses Päckchen nach Amerika schicken. Was kostet das, bitte?*

Employee: *Moment mal! 500 Gramm nach Amerika kostet leider DM 20, 50. Füllen Sie bitte das Formular aus.*

Customer: *Formular? Warum denn das?*

Employee: *Sie müssen sagen, was in dem Päckchen ist, und wieviel es gekostet hat.*

Customer: *Ach so!*

German Higher

This extract comes from the end of a 'Higher' test. A little detective work is needed with this recording; we are not *told* who Kurt is (question 2), but you can work it out.

QUESTIONS

Frau Theimann has just fetched her younger sister Emmi from the railway station. On the way back to Frau Theimann's house they have a conversation. Frau Theimann speaks first. Listen carefully and then answer *in English*.

1 Why did Emmi decide to spend some days with her sister?

2 Who is Kurt?

3 What is he doing at the moment?

4 Where are Emmi's children?

5 On what day does Emmi propose to return home?

6 Why on that particular day?

7 Why does she intend to travel in the morning?

(Southern Examining Group)

TRANSCRIPT OF RECORDING

Frau T: *Wie schön, dich wieder bei uns zu haben!*

Emmi: *Ja. Weil so schönes Wetter war, entschloß ich mich, ein paar Tage zu euch zu fahren.*

Frau T: *Und was macht Kurt in der Zwischenzeit?*

Emmi: *Es trifft sich gut. Er ist gerade auf einer Geschäftsreise nach München.*

Frau T: *Und die Kinder?*

Emmi: *Sie wohnen solange bei Kurts Mutter. Sie freut sich, wenn sie sie einmal haben kann.*

Frau T: *Die Kinder sind immer sehr gern bei ihr.*

Emmi: *Ja. Sie sind von ihr ganz verwöhnt.*

Frau T: *Wie lange hast du vor, bei uns zu bleiben?*

Emmi: *Kurt kommt erst nächsten Dienstag nach Hause zurück. Am besten fahre ich am Dienstagmorgen ab, damit ich am Nachmittag noch einige Besorgungen machen kann.*

Frau T: *Hoffentlich bleibt das Wetter so schön, damit du ein paar angenehme Tage bei uns verbringen kannst.*

ANSWERS

French Basic

(a) Saturday **(b)** go to the beach or the country **(c)** it's fine **(d)** She's not particularly bothered about going out with the boy. (She agrees to go maybe, if it's fine, but if not she'd just as soon stay at home.)

French Higher

(a) In a big hotel. (You obviously need to say that she was in a hotel, and it's a good idea to mention that it was big; in a small hotel she wouldn't have had such a problem. You *don't* need to give the name of the hotel; it's irrelevant to the experience; and you won't get any extra marks for mentioning London, because that's in the introduction.) **(b)** About twelve. (Twelve is the main point here, *une douzaine d'années*, not to be confused with *il y a une dixaine d'années*, 'about ten years ago'. 'About' is conveyed by *aine*; she doesn't remember *exactly* how old she was, only that she hadn't been learning English long.) **(c)** She got shut/locked out of her room. (Not out of the *hotel*.) **(d)** She went to the desk/office and tried to explain.

Your criterion for what to include in your answers should be, 'If I were telling this to a friend, would he now understand adequately?' Here are the same questions and answers set out as a chat:

'Where did she say she was?'
'In a big hotel.'
'How old was she?'
'She must have been about 12.'
'What happened to her?'
'The door of her room shut behind her so she was locked out.'
'So what did she do?'
'She managed to get to the desk and explain.'

These answers are natural and full. You must judge whether *your* answers would have told the story sufficiently.

German Basic

(a) Send a parcel to America. (This question carries two marks, and you need to mention both 'parcel' or 'package' and 'America' to get both.) **(b)** 20.50 Marks. (Not 500: that was the weight in grammes. Not 250 or 205 Marks − you should know enough about Germany to pick a reasonable price.) **(c)** What's in the parcel, and how much it cost. (Again, there are two marks so you must make both points.)

German Higher

1 Because the weather was so fine. **2** Emmi's husband. **3** He is on a business trip. **4** With their grandmother. **5** On Tuesday. **6** Because that's when Kurt returns home. **7** To do some shopping/To see some things (1 point) in the afternoon (1 point).

READING: HINTS AND TIPS

There's a lot of common sense involved in the 'Reading' test. You can often get clues from the English questions themselves, or from the layout and design. For example, look at part of the front page of a Dutch newspaper opposite. Suppose that with the aid of a dictionary, you intend to find out:

what date the paper was published;
what the main news stories are;
who the table-tennis champion is;
and what's in tomorrow's paper.

Clearly you don't have to read every word to find out; by using your experience of newspaper layout, and the photos, you can go straight to the relevant parts of the page.

75

Here is a cutting from the same front page.

Perioden met zon

In de ochtend eerst nog hier en daar mistbanken, overigens droog weer en perioden met zon. Middagtemperatuur ongeveer 6 graden.

You can guess what it's about from the picture symbol, so you know the meaning of the word **weer**. This tells you what sort of vocabulary to expect. You know English, and Dutch is related to English. Read the paragraph intelligently, then try some GCSE-type questions:

What kind of weather will there be today? — — — — —

What will the weather be like early in the morning? — — — — — —

Will the rest of the day be wet or dry? — — — — — —

When will temperatures reach six degrees? — — — — — —

If you can answer without knowing a word of Dutch, think what you'll be able to do in a language you've been studying for years!

READING PRACTICE

These basic rules will help you to tackle the exam questions:

1 look *briefly* at the *text* and read *all through* the *questions* (The questions will often give you clues about the text.);

2 look through the text again, ignoring anything you don't understand, until you come to the parts which seem to answer the questions;

3 read each question again carefully, and study the relevant part of the text with all the memory, wit and common sense you have, in an effort to understand the *exact* meaning of that part of the text.

Now tackle some specimen exam tasks. (Answers on page 81.)

French Basic

Before you start on the specimen task below, here are a few reminders:

* You don't need to read it all — skim for what you need. No. **19**: look for prices. **20** and **23**: find the regulations. **22**: the words 'six o'clock' aren't there by accident; skim for times. **24**: look for dates.

* Profit from words which are almost the same in French and English: *tente, caravane, adulte, véhicule, attacher, non-respect, départ*.

* Watch out for endings which have a meaning (see page 41): *entrée, cuisiné, numéroté, campeur, visiblement*.

* Look out for known words within longer words: **numéro**té, **emplace**ment, **cuisiné**.

* There are some words which you just need to have learnt: *laisser, bureau, ouvert, jusqu'à*.

* Use what you know about France: 5,00 = five francs (not five hundred francs); know the 24-hour clock.

You are touring France with a friend by car and you decide to stop for a night at the 'Camping du Puits d'Enfer'. You arrive early in the evening.

Look at the following questions and answer them in English by referring to the camping site notice.

19 How much more must you pay for a night for

    (a) pitching your tent?   ...... F

    (b) yourself and your friend? ...... F

    (c) your car?   ...... F

20 According to the regulations, what should you do with the number given to you at reception?

21 You are worried about leaving your passport and money in your tent. What can you do with them?

22 It's six o'clock and you want to eat something hot. You have cooking equipment with you but no gas left.
What two options are open to you?

23 What happens if you do not observe the rules?

24 When you leave, you want to book a camping site for next May. Give two reasons why this is not possible.

(Midland Examining Group)

CAMPING DU PUITS D'ENFER

85100 — LE CHÂTEAU — D'OLONNE

Tél: (51) 32-73-19

Terrain Classé * NN — 500 emplacements — Arrêté préfectoral du 19 juillet 1977

OUVERT:	du 1er JUIN au 30 SEPTEMBRE

OUVERT: du 1er JUIN au 30 SEPTEMBRE

Aucune réservation n'est possible.

TARIFS: <u>Redevances journalières:</u>

Adulte .... 5,00 F

Enfant de moins de 7 ans .... 3,00 F

Emplacement pour la tente .... 2,50 F

Véhicule .... 2,00 F

La redevance journalière s'entend pour chaque période de 24 heures décomptée de midi à midi.

BUREAU: ouvert de 8 à 20 heures

COMMERCES: Épicerie libre-service: ouverte de 8 à 13 h. et de 17 à 19 h. Boissons, Glaces, Alimentation, Bouteilles de gaz . . .

Plats cuisinés (froids et chauds) servis jusqu'à 20 h 30.

COURRIER: arrivée et départ vers 10 heures

TRANSPORT: Un service d'autocars pour Château d'Olonne dessert le camp toutes les heures, sur l'heure.

RAPPEL DU RÈGLEMENT À OBSERVER:

— A votre inscription, il vous est remis une plaquette numérotée que vous devez attacher visiblement à l'entrée de votre tente ou caravane.

— Un badge vous est donné pour votre véhicule à coller au milieu et en haut du pare-brise.

— La circulation des automobiles dans le camp doit se faire au maximum de 20 km/heure et de 7 heures à 22 heures. Circulation interdite des motos dans le camp.

— Il vous est possible de laisser vos objets de valeur au Bureau.

— Les chiens et autres animaux doivent être tenus en laisse.

— Le téléphone et le haut-parleur du Camping sont réservés aux cas urgents: appel d'un docteur, etc.

— Tous feux sont interdits.

Le non-respect du règlement entraîne le départ immédiat du campeur.

MERCI ET BON SÉJOUR

French Higher

The newspaper cutting opposite would be daunting if you had to translate, or even understand, every word. Luckily, you can ignore the map, completely, and ignore much of the text, selectively. In fact, you can answer all the questions just by picking out the English look-alikes: *Pyrénées, Alpes, Méditerranée, centre, intérieur*; and knowing the meanings of just ten words: *couvert, pluvieux, beau, brume, gelée, vent, nord, ouest, fort, Manche*. If you aren't sure of all of those, you can look for clues in the surrounding sentence. You aren't expected to be an expert in French geography, so it doesn't matter if you've never heard of *Vendée, Berry* or the *Vosges*. However, you *are* expected to have discovered during your years of studying French and France that the Mediterranean is in the south, and that *la Manche* refers to the Channel.

Temps doux mais gris quelques éclaircies dans le Midi

En France aujourd'hui

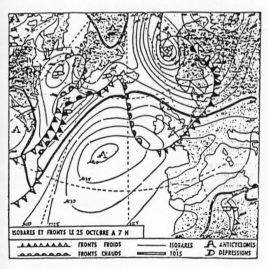

ISOBARES ET FRONTS LE 25 OCTOBRE A 7 H

FRONTS FROIDS — ISOBARES ⬩ANTICYCLONES
FRONTS CHAUDS — 1015 D DÉPRESSIONS

Une étroite bande de temps couvert et pluvieux affectera encore ce matin nos régions situées des Pyrénées au nord des Alpes avant de se désagréger sur place au cours de la journée.

A son avant, il fera beau près de la Méditerranée.

A son arrière, des éclaircies se développeront temporairement, mais le ciel redeviendra rapidement très nuageux près de la Manche, puis de la Vendée au Berry et aux Vosges, où se produiront de faibles pluies éparses. De nombreuses brumes matinales ne se dissiperont qu'assez lentement du nordest au centre et à l'Aquitaine.

Après quelques faibles gelées matinales dans l'intérieur, les températures maximales s'élèveront partout.

Les vents, modérés de nordouest en général, deviendront assez forts d'ouest, près de la Manche.

Describe the morning weather:

   (i) From the Pyrenees to the Alps. (2 marks)

   (ii) In the South of France. (1 mark)

   (iii) In central France. (2 marks)

   (iv) What will happen to the NW winds on the Channel coast? (2 marks)

German Basic

Remember that you don't need to understand every word. Don't panic if you don't know *heiter* — you don't *need* to for these questions.

Read the following weather forecast for Nordrhein-Westfalen (NRW) from a German newspaper, then select the most suitable answer to each question.

HEITER

Ein Hoch mit Kern über der Nordsee ist für NRW wetterbestimmend. Vorhersage für heute: Heiter bis wolkig und trocken. Höchsttemperaturen um 23, in den Hochlagen von Sauerland und Eifel 19 Grad. Tiefsttemperaturen in der Nacht 14 bis 10 Grad.

Weitere Aussichten: Auch am Wochenende trocken und warm.

1 **What is affecting today's weather?**
  A **Cold winds from the North Sea.**
  B **A low pressure area over NRW.**
  C **Thick clouds over the Sauerland and the Eifel.**
  D **A high pressure area over the North Sea.**

2 **What is likely to be the highest temperature during the night?**
  A **19 degrees;** *B* **14 degrees;** *C* **23 degrees;** *D* **10 degrees**

3 **What kind of weather can we expect at the weekend?**
  A **cold** *B* **cloudy** *C* **dry** *D* **wet**

(Southern Examining Group)

German Higher

Before you start the specimen exam task opposite:

* As usual, read through all the questions. Question **3** gives you a lot of help with question **1**!

* Watch out for short words hiding in long words: in here are *Waffe*, 'weapon' (remember that German **f** is often English 'p'); *Maske* and *nehmen* (to take) — which practically tell you the story on their own!

* Look out for prefixes like **vor** (before): *vorgestern, am Tag vorher*; or **ge** indicating a past participle; and suffixes like **iert** for English 'ed'.

* Compound words, however long, (*Geldschrank, dunkelgrün*) should give you no trouble.

* Don't let endings or vowel changes distract you from the meaning of words like *Pistolen, Männer, Räuber, gestohlen, Polizei.*

Here is a news item from the *Süddeutsche Zeitung*. Read it carefully and then answer, *in English*, the questions which follow.

CASINO IN SAN REMO ÜBERFALLEN

Vorgestern haben zwei mit Pistolen bewaffnete Männer das Spiel-casino in San Remo an der italienischen Riviera überfallen. Die mit roten Tüchern maskierten Räuber drangen in das Büro des Casinos ein, zwangen zwei Angestellte und einen Wächter sich auf den Boden zu legen, öffneten den Geldschrank mit einem vom Wächter entnom-menen Schlüssel und flohen in einem Auto. Ein dunkelgrüner Mercedes, der schon am Tag vorher gestohlen worden war, wird von der Polizei gesucht.

Süddeutsche Zeitung, Montag, den 15. Oktober 1984)

1 **What incident is reported in this news-item? (1 mark)**

2 **What were the employees made to do? (1 mark)**

3 **How were the criminals able to open the safe? (2 marks)**

4 **What are the police looking for and why? (2 marks)**

(Southern Examining Group)

ANSWERS

Dutch:
1 Sunny periods. **2** Misty. **3** Dry (*droog weer*). **4** Midday.

French Basic
19 (a) 2.50 **19 (b)** 10 **19 (c)** 2 **20** Attach it where it can be seen at the entrance to the tent or caravan. **21** Leave them at the office. **22** Buy some gas at the shop; buy some ready-cooked food (a take-away meal). **23** Must leave at once. **24** It's only open June–September; it is not possible to book.

French Higher
(i) Overcast/rain. (*couvert*: 'covered'; i.e. 'sky covered with clouds'; *pluvieux*, from *pluie*: 'rain'. Or, since you know it's something to do with weather, you could have guessed the meaning from your know-ledge of *il pleut*.) (ii) Fine. (*Beau* near the Mediterranean.) (iii) Misty and frosty. (To get 'misty' you needed to home in on the word *centre*, then look for a weather word in the sentence. If you didn't know *brume*, you could guess it from the phrase *brumes matinales se dissi-peront*: 'morning ? will dissipate'. 'Foggy' or 'hazy' are also correct. To get 'frosty' you had to notice the word *intérieur* and find a nearby

81

weather phrase. If you'd never met *gelée* before, you might guess it if you remembered that *il gèle* means 'it's freezing'.) (iv) Will change to become stronger and from the west. (If you wondered whether *modérés de nord-ouest* or *forts d'ouest* gave the right answer, you need to notice the future ending of *deviendront:* 'will become'.)

German Basic

1:D Answer *A* can be ruled out because there is no sign in the text of words meaning 'cold winds'. 'Low', *tief*, and 'cloudy', *wolkig*, are mentioned, but not in connection with the place-names in *B* and *C*. Confirm *D* by noticing *Hoch* near the word *Nordsee,* and remembering that **ch** in German is often 'gh' in English. **2:** *B* The clue-word here is *Nacht* (night): **ch**/'gh' again. **3:**C Clue-word: *trocken*, one of the many words where German **t** is English 'd'.

German Higher

1 Armed robbery. **2** To lie on the floor. (You need to locate the word for 'employees', plural, in the text, which must be *zwei Angestellte*. To find out what they were made to do, look at *zu legen*. If you've forgotten its meaning, remember that German *g* is often English 'i', which may remind you of 'lie'. Lie where? *Auf den Boden.* You should know that *auf* is 'on', so if necessary you could guess *Boden*: where else would they be made to lie but on the floor?) **3** With a key taken from the watchman/security guard. (The German says literally, 'with a from the watchman taken-away key'.) **4** A dark-green Mercedes, because it had been stolen.

SPEAKING: HINTS AND TIPS

Well before the day of the oral test, your teacher should prepare you so that you know the answers to these points of procedure:
* Who will the examiner be?
* Will I meet him/her beforehand?
* How many role-plays do I have to do?
* Will the examiner intervene with an unexpected development in the role-play?
* How long will the conversation last?
* Will there be anything else besides role-play and conversation?
* What order will things happen in?
* How much preparation time will there be?
* Will the examiner repeat or rephrase if I don't understand?
* And if so, will I lose marks?

It's to be hoped that you will have had a 'mock' speaking test which is as similar as possible to the real thing, and plenty of practice in class.

Even if that's not possible in your class, you must still be prepared. Remember that there won't be any surprises in the test because it will be restricted to the settings and topics on the syllabus, so if you've practised as described in Section 2 of this book until you can say everything there without too much stumbling and hesitation, you can face the examiner with confidence.

Try the specimen tasks below, ideally with someone who can assess your performance. If nobody is available, talking into a tape-recorder is a good idea; listen to yourself afterwards, and try to judge yourself objectively. A suggested scoring scale is given underneath.

CONVERSATION PRACTICE

Have you checked from the 'Conversation' sections (French, page 31; German, page 49) that you've got something to say on all the set topics? Saying, 'Yes' and 'No' alone won't do. If you're ready, imagine that you are being asked these questions in the language you are studying. Don't prepare your answers or hesitate too long after reading each question; pretend it's a genuine interview and that you are expected to reply reasonably quickly.

Basic

This sample of the sort of questions you might be asked is an extract from the examiner's notes. *You* won't see the questions written down, you'll just hear them in the foreign language. Notice that they include questions on your future intentions and on past events.

> **Do you get up early in the mornings?**
> **What time?**
> **Do you have breakfast?**
> **What foods do you like?**
> **Do you have dinner at school?**
> **Do you go out at weekends?**
> **What do you normally do on Saturday mornings?**
> **What are you going to do this Saturday afternoon?**
> **Do you go away on holiday?**
> **Where do you go? Do you like it?**
> **Did you go there last year?**
> **Tell me something about what you did.**

(Midland Examining Group)

Where did you come on this scale?

1 Could just about give very simple answers to some of the questions.

2 Could attempt quite a few questions, but a native speaker would have had trouble understanding the answers.

3 Could attempt most questions, including those about the past and future. A native speaker *who was really trying* would have understood the answers.

4 As for *3*, but a native speaker would have understood *easily*.

5 Could answer clearly and with few errors even questions about the past and future.

(based on Southern Examining Group guidelines)

Higher

You will see from the following extract from the examiner's notes that for 'Higher Speaking' you are expected to say what you *would* do as well as what you *have* done or *will* do, and that you should be prepared to give your opinion.

How do you get to school in the mornings?
 Which subjects do you like doing?
 What do you like about them?
What do you do in your spare time?
 How will you spend next weekend?
Do you normally go away on holiday?
 What did you do on holiday last summer?
 Have you ever been abroad?
 Where did you go?
 What did you do?
Is there any country or place you would like to visit?
 Why?
What do you hope to do when you leave school?

(Midland Examining Group)

Where did you come on this scale?

1 Very little to say, and most of that unintelligible.

2 Sometimes lost for words and unintelligible, but at other times communicated adequately and fairly accurately.

3 Mostly communicated well but with occasional muddles, especially on the more demanding questions.

4 Communicated quite complicated ideas effectively, but with a few mistakes or hesitations.

5 Had no trouble communicating quite complicated ideas. If there were any mistakes, they didn't confuse the listener.

(from Southern Examining Group's guidelines)

ROLE-PLAY PRACTICE

On the day of the test, practise aloud during your preparation time, however silly you feel. Remember to use *vous/Sie* to adults and *tu/du* to teenagers.

Basic

Prepare these two role-plays for a few moments, then try them out. As for 'Conversation', try to say them either to a person or to a tape-recorder. In the test, the examiner would play the part of the other person involved, and would have his/her own script.

If you are stuck with the first role-play, revise the 'Role-play' sentences on *illness* and *shopping* in Section 2 of this book.

You are in a chemist's shop. Your examiner is the shop-keeper.

1 Ask if the shop has something for insect-bites.

2 Say that you also have a headache.

3 Ask how much your purchases cost.

(London and East Anglia Group)

If you are stuck with the second role-play, you will get some help from the 'Role-play' sections on *post office, phone, bank* and *lost property* and *sightseeing*.

You are in a bank. Your examiner is the bank clerk.

1 Check that you are at the right counter to change money.

2 Say that you wish to change £50 sterling into French francs/ German Marks.

3 When asked for your passport, apologise and explain that you have left your passport at the hotel.

4 Ask if the bank will be open tomorrow.

(London and East Anglia Group)

Possible answers are on page 86.

Higher

Prepare the card below, bearing in mind that the examiner/shop-assistant will intervene with some extra points which aren't on the card.

You are in a clothes shop. Your examiner is the shop-assistant.

1 Point out a type of tee-shirt in the shop that you would like to try on.

2 Say that you are not sure of your size – it might be 42.

3 Agree to the shop-assistant's suggestion and choose a colour.

4 You are in a hurry, so react appropriately to the asssistant's next question.

5 Say you will take the tee-shirt, check the price, and if you are happy with it, pay.

Examiner's interventions, which you don't know until you hear them:

after your number 2, you are told that they are out of size 42, and will you try a 44?

after your number 3, you are asked if you'd like to go to a changing room.

(London and East Anglia Group)

ANSWERS

There are no 'right answers' because there are so many different ways of conveying the same message. These are suggestions, in French and German.

Basic: First role-play

1 Avez-vous quelque chose pour les piqûres d'insecte?

Haben Sie etwas gegen Stiche?

2 J'ai aussi mal à la tête.

Ich habe auch Kopfschmerzen.

3 C'est combien?

Was kostet das?

Basic: Second role-play

1 Est-ce que je peux changer de l'argent ici?

Kann ich hier Geld wechseln?

2 Je voudrais changer 50 livres sterling en francs français.

Ich möchte 50 Pfund in D-Mark wechseln.

3 Ah non, pardon, j'ai laissé mon passeport à l'hôtel.

Ach, Entschuldigung, ich habe meinen Paß im Hotel vergessen.

*4 Est-ce que la banque est
    ouverte demain?*

*Ist die Sparkasse morgen
geöffnet?*

How did you get on? Score each instruction on each role-play:

   0 **No message conveyed, or message unintelligible to a native speaker.**

   1 **Message only partly conveyed, or hard to understand.**

   2 **Message fully conveyed, even if not perfectly correct.**

                  (from Southern Examining Group's guidelines)

Higher

*1 Est-ce que je peux/Je voudrais
    essayer un de ces T-shirts-là(?)*

*Kann ich eins von den T-shirts
dort anprobieren?*

*2 Je ne sais pas exactement − c'est
    peut-être quarante-deux.*

*Ich weiß nicht genau, ich glaube
zweiundvierzig.*

*3 Oui, ça va/je vais l'essayer.
    Donnez-moi celui-là en
    (colour)/donnez-m'en un en
    (colour), s'il vous plaît.*

*Ja, das ist in Ordnung, das
probiere ich an. Geben Sie mir
das bitte in (colour).*

*4 Non, merci, je suis pressé(e). Je
    vais le mettre/essayer ici,
    comme ça.*

*Nein danke. Ich bin in Eile. Ich
probiere es so an.*

*5 Oui, je le prends. C'est combien,
    s'il vous plaît?*

*Ja, ich nehme es. Wieviel
macht das, bitte?*

6 (Pay if you are happy with
    price.)

(Pay if you are happy with the
price.)

Score your performance using the same scale as for 'Higher Conversation'.

WRITING: HINTS AND TIPS

The five exam Groups set various 'Writing' tasks, with slightly differing mark schemes. It's up to you and your teacher to find out from the syllabus, well before the exam, exactly what to expect. Can you complete these details for 'Basic' or for 'Basic' and 'Higher', according to which you are taking?

1 What sorts of tasks are there? (e.g. informal letters? picture essays?)

. . . .

. . . .

Prepare accordingly. For letters, learn the beginning and ending formulae. Essays: learn your past tenses.

2 Is there any choice? If so, give details.

. . . .

. . . .

If you *know* there's a choice (e.g. *either* formal letter *or* picture essay), you can safely concentrate on one of them.

3 How many words should you write for each task?

. . . .

. . . .

Now find out what that many words look like in your handwriting.

4 How long should you spend on each question?

. . . .

. . . .

As in a written exam in *any* subject, *plan* your time and *stick* to your plan.

5 Are you allowed to write a rough version first? . . . .

If 'yes', always make a plan or notes *in the foreign language*, then a rough version, then the final copy.

WRITING PRACTICE

If you've answered the questions above, you'll know which of the following specimen tasks are the sorts of things you'll have to do, and how long you should spend on each, from first thoughts to final version. Answer them, including a rough version, *sticking to a suitable length and timing*. (Where the instructions say 'German' or 'French', substitute the other language if necessary.) Even if you can't get them marked, the practice in planning and timing will be invaluable.

No answers are given in this section because there's no such thing as a 'right' answer in the 'Writing' test; there are poor answers, good answers, brilliant answers, and everything else in between. It's up to you to choose the words and phrases which show what you can do.

If you happen to know the details of the mark schemes provided by your exam Group, use them instead of the mark schemes quoted here. Usually, the marks are divided between *what* you say (communication) and *how well* you say it. When you've attempted the tasks, use the mark scheme to try to assess honestly whether you would score the points given for transmitting the message. The first thing to do is to be brutal — cross out all the sentences where you've invented words in the hope that they exist, or used English words for lack of foreign ones, or left blanks in the sentences because you don't know how to say something. Almost certainly such sentences would make no sense to a native speaker, so they're worthless. Next be equally brutal where you've made up the word-count with long lists of names of your favourite bands, your seventeen cousins or all the places you've visited. Then look at what's left and decide if you've really conveyed all the messages required.

To get a mark for the *quality* of your writing, you need to ask a teacher to look at it.

Basic

Messages

Write a message in German of 20–30 words, based on the following situation:
You arrive in Koblenz with a school party. You call on your German pen-friend who lives in Koblenz. She/he is out and so you write a message including the following information:

(a) You arrived yesterday by train.   (1 item)

(b) You are staying at the youth hostel.   (1 item)

(c) You can meet your friend at 3 o'clock tomorrow. Suggest a meeting-place. (1 item)

(Southern Examining Group)

Mark scheme: for each item,

3 marks for transmission of the message even with minor error;

2 marks if there are some errors but the German can still be understood;

1 mark if there is a lot of error or half the message is missing;

0 if the message was not transmitted or cannot be understood.

Note that this mark scheme gives 0 if the message wasn't conveyed. For **(c)**, for instance, if you write a long, well-spelt and grammatically accurate sentence, yet the word you've chosen for the meeting-place can't be understood, you get nothing. Which is fair enough, because the friend wouldn't turn up, so it was useless. On the other hand, you could get three points, even if there's the odd mistake, provided you've conveyed the key ideas of 'meet – 3 p.m. – tomorrow – place'. This doesn't mean that accuracy doesn't matter. It means that communication matters more.

Informal letters

Before you start: are you *sure* you've learnt the letter-writing rules perfectly? No cheating!

Remember that informal letters are letters to a friend, so try to make your style friendly. They are often based on the conversation topics on the syllabus, so if you're stuck with this letter, you might get some ideas from the key sentences in the 'Conversation' section about *home* (local town and recent events), *school* and *leisure.*

Write a letter in German of about 100 words to a friend, mentioning the following points:

(a) Thank him/her for his/her letter. (1 item)

(b) Explain the arrangements for meeting her/him from the plane and for getting her/him to your house. (2 items)

(c) Say you are enclosing a town plan. (1 item)

(d) Give details of what there is to do in your town, naming at least two things that you hope he/she likes doing. (3 items)

(e) Give details of what you have been doing recently both at school and out of school. (2 items)

Remember to begin and end the letter correctly. (1 item)

(Southern Examining Group)

Mark scheme: You can use the same mark scheme as for 'Messages' above, but this time there are ten items to score instead of three. Notice how the marks are distributed: you've got to cover *all* the items to get full marks, and you can't get *more* than the marks it says for any part of the letter. So if you get carried away and write so much in answer to **(b)** that you've got no time or space for **(c)**, **(d)** and **(e)**, you're throwing away 60% of the marks for this task.

Higher

Formal letters

You're not trying this before learning the formulae, are you?

Formal letters are often based on the role-play topics on the syllabus. If you're stuck with this letter, get some ideas from the *lost property* sentences in the 'Role-play' section.

> **On returning from your holiday in France, your mother discovers that she has left her camera in the hotel where you spent the last night. Write to the hotel, in French, to ask if they have found it. Give all the relevant details (e.g. describe the camera, say where your mother left it, give the dates of your stay). Write between 90–100 words, excluding your address and the date.**
>
> **Your letter is addressed to the Hôtel Molière, rue Molière, 75001 PARIS/Hotel Diehl, Hohenpfad 17, 28 Bremen.**
>
> **(Northern Examining Association)**

Mark scheme based on the Southern Examining Group's guidelines:

> One third of the marks for *conveying the messages* completely, and clearly enough to be understood by a sympathetic native speaker.
>
> One third for *accuracy*. (Verbs and adjectives should have the right endings, word order should be correct, spelling should be careful, with none of those French accents that manage to point in both directions at once, or umlauts written very faintly in the hope that the reader will consider them optional.)
>
> One third for *quality*. (If you're a high-flyer, here's your chance to prove it. But you've only got a hundred or so words to do it in. Make the most of them. If you can do so without making a mess of it, write complex sentences rather than baby simple sentences, show your range of vocabulary instead of using the same words twice, and where you know more than one way of expressing the same idea, choose the one which does the job best.)

At 'Higher' level, it's no longer possible to get full marks for communication alone.

In 'Higher Writing', you are likely to have to read a document in French/
German and respond in writing. This example uses a genuine cutting
from a French newspaper as a basis for story-telling. A made-up German
equivalent has been added for those taking German.

LA VOITURE EST TOU-JOURS LÀ MAIS LES PNEUS ONT DISPARUS!

En retrouvant l'autre matin sa voiture qu'il avait garée le long de l'avenue Montrose, M. David Pearson, vacancier britannique, a eu la désagréable surprise de constater que les quatre pneus avaient tout simplement disparu!
(Nice-Martin, 29.8.84)

DAS AUTO IST NOCH DA, ABER DIE REIFEN SIND VERSCHWUNDEN!

Als Herr David Pearson, ein britisher Tourist, neulich zu seinem Auto zurückkam, das er in der Martinistraße geparkt hatte, fand er zu seiner unangenehmen Überraschung, daß seine vier Reifen einfach verschwunden waren!

Imagine that you are one of Mr Pearson's children. Write, in French, a letter of about 100 words to a French friend telling him or her about this incident and what happened afterwards.

This can be scored using the 'Higher' mark scheme which was quoted
for 'Formal Letters'.

The story relates an incident in the past, so to tell it sensibly you will
need to know your past tenses. If you're taking 'Higher Writing', face
the fact that you've got to study the rules for forming past tenses, and
learn those verb tables by heart.